Totally Cool
JOURNALS,
NOTEBOOKS
& DIARIES

Totally Cool
JOURNALS,
NOTEBOOKS
& DIARIES

Janet Pensiero

Sterling Publishing Co., Inc.
New York

Prolific Impressions Production Staff:

Editor in Chief: Mickey Baskett
Copy Editor: Phyllis Mueller
Graphics: Dianne Miller, Karen Turpin
Styling: Kirsten Jones
Photography: Jerry Mucklow
Administration: Jim Baskett

Every effort has been made to insure that the information presented is accurate. Since we have no control over physical conditions, individual skills, or chosen tools and products, the publisher disclaims any liability for injuries, losses, untoward results, or any other damages which may result from the use of the information in this book. Thoroughly read the instructions for all products used to complete the projects in this book, paying particular attention to all cautions and warnings shown for that product to ensure their proper and safe use.

Library of Congress Cataloging-in-Publication Data Available

Pensiero, Janet.
  Totally cool journals, notebooks & diaries / Janet Pensiero.
    p. cm.
  ISBN 1-4027-0341-4
  1. book design--Juvenile literature. 2. Blank-books--Juvenile literature. 3. Handicraft--Juvenile literature. I. Title: Totally cool journals, notebooks and diaries. II. Title.
Z116.A3P46 2003
686--dc21
                          2003002682

10 9 8 7 6 5 4 3 2 1

Published by Sterling Publishing Co., Inc.
387 Park Avenue South, New York, N.Y. 10016

© 2003 by Prolific Impressions, Inc.

Produced by Prolific Impressions, Inc.
160 South Candler St., Decatur, GA 30030

Distributed in Canada by Sterling Publishing
c/o Canadian Manda Group, One Atlantic Avenue, Suite 105
Toronto, Ontario, Canada M6K 3E7
Distributed in Great Britain and Europe by Chris Lloyd at Orca Book
Services, Stanley House, Fleets Lane, Poole BH15 3AJ, England
Distributed in Australia by Capricorn Link (Australia) Pty. Ltd.
P.O. Box 704, Windsor, NSW 2756 Australia

Printed in China
All rights reserved
Sterling ISBN 1-4027-0341-4

Acknowledgements

While putting this book together, I had help and support from some great craft suppliers:

• Plaid Enterprises/All Night Media, www.plaidonline.com (stamps, punches, charms, tags, dried flowers)

• Hero Arts (stamps, ink, origami paper)

• Magnetsource.com (magnets)

• Beacon Adhesives (Kids Choice glue, Craft Foam glue)

• Aldastar (chenille pom-poms)

• Grafix (funky fur, funky film, vellum)

• Sulyn (glitter glue, chenille stems)

• Loose Ends (handmade paper)

• Wilde-Ideas.com (punch-and-disc binding system)

• Two Busy Moms (patterned paper and stickers)

• Stampinfunaddict (stamps and supplies).

I also had the terrific support and encouragement of many friends, especially Chris Mullen and her photogenic kids.

Most of all, I'd like to thank my family: Frances, Jan, Matt and Kate Carr, and especially my parents Ben and Angie Pensiero for their years of love and support.

Last but not least, thanks to my editor Mickey Baskett, who refused to give up on this book proposal, and who has put it together beautifully.

Table of Contents

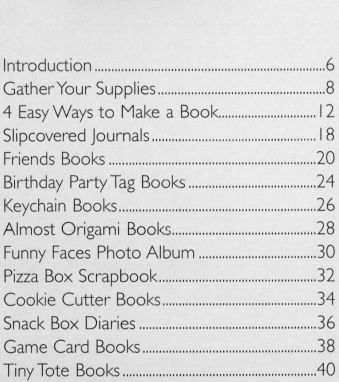

If you've ever kept a journal or written a story for a school project, you know how much work can go into the content of a book. But did you ever think that the book itself – the cover and the pages – can be as special as the words and pictures you put in it?

In this book, I'm showing you some great ideas for making fun, special, cool books that you can fill up with your special stuff, and I've included some fun ideas for

decorating the pages, too. You'll see some projects that look like regular books – they have covers, pages, and bindings. Others are a little different, but as long as there are pages bound together, it's a book!

Of course, you don't have to make your books exactly like the ones shown here. Feel free to experiment and improvise. Try different papers and materials. Or make the pages weird shapes. If you don't have a hole punch, you can staple or tape the pages together; if you're in a hurry, try decorating the cover of a purchased book to make it your personal creation.

The next time you have an idea or an event you want to celebrate with a special book or journal, use these projects as guides and inspiration.

Janet Pensiero

Gather Your Supplies

Shopping for materials can be a fun part of any project. Places you might want to visit include craft stores, fabric stores, thrift shops, hardware stores, office supply stores, specialty scrapbook stores, and everything-for-a-dollar stores. And, of course, there's the Internet, which is filled with lots of arts and crafts websites.

Don't forget recycled stuff! Book projects are a great place to use items you rescue from the trash, like odd-sized pieces of paper, cardboard boxes, scraps of wrapping paper, old pieces of jewelry, paper bags, and magazine pages.

Tools

- Scissors, a ruler, and a pencil are needed to make all of these projects.
- Decorative scissors are fun to use. They come in a variety of different designs, and can add some jazz to even a simple book.
- A hole punch is necessary for many of the bindings. I used round hole punches in two sizes, 1/4" and 1/8". You could also use tiny shapes like stars or hearts.
- Punch-and-disc binding system, which consists of a binding punch, a guide, and discs in a variety of sizes and colors, is easy to use and will let you bind almost anything into a book. You can find these in scrapbook stores or on the internet.
- Stapler and staples also can be used for binding.

Paper for Covers

- Posterboard – it's easy to find, it's inexpensive, and it comes in a lot of colors. Recycled paperboard, like the boxes that snack foods and candy come in, and cardboard, like pizza boxes, can also used.
- Clear plastic file folders and envelopes and paper file folders are great for book projects. They come in lots of colors and are easy to cut. With the plastic ones you can create wonderful see through designs.
- Other cover materials could be vinyl tablecloths, paper bags, or fabric.

continued on page 10

Scissor Safety

- Grown-up help should be used when working with scissors.
- Very young children should not be left unsupervised when working with scissors.
- Blunt point scissors are the best kind to use for kid's crafts.
- Don't walk or run with scissors in your hand.
- When handing scissors to a friend, hold the pointed end in your hand, with the handle end facing your friend.
- Scissors are for cutting only paper, thread, or ribbon. They are not meant for cutting things such as wire or wood, they will become dull.

✎ Paper for Pages

- Copy paper is my favorite. It can be found in office supply stores, dollar stores, large drugstores, and even in the supermarket! It comes in lots of colors and is not expensive.
- Index cards are a great size for pages, come in colors, and are lined. I used both 3x5 and 4x6 sizes.
- Blank newsprint, construction paper, brown kraft paper, tags, and even envelopes can be used as pages.
- Card stock can be found in larger sheets. It can also be used for covers.

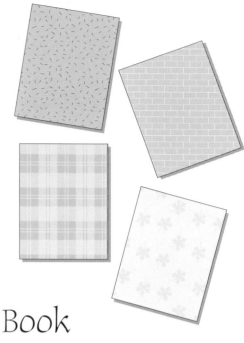

✎ Items for Decorating Your Book

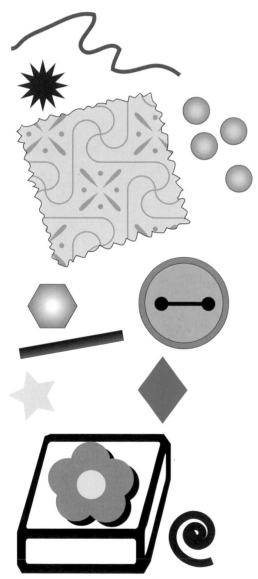

- Decorative and patterned papers. Stores that sell scrapbook supplies usually have a good selection. The paper comes in 8-1/2" x 11" or 12" x 12" sheets. (You'll find that one sheet of patterned paper goes a long way.) Origami paper sheets, which are smaller, have wonderful intricate designs.
- Handmade paper can be found in most art supply and craft stores. (Sometimes people call it "crunchy paper" because it looks like there are crunchy things like leaves and twigs imbedded in it.) It can cost a little more, but it will make your projects look extra special.
- Don't forget about wrapping paper like gift wrap, butcher paper, and kraft paper, and recycled paper like the Sunday comics.
- Craft foam is easy to use, doesn't cost much, and comes in great colors. You can glue it yourself or buy it with adhesive on the back. It's also available with some neat patterns worked into the foam. It's easy to measure and trace on craft foam, and it can be cut with scissors. There is also special glue exclusively for craft foam – you spread it on areas to be glued, let it set up, and stick the pieces together.
- Fabrics of all kinds, including felt and plush felt, plush fabrics, or and fake fur add dimension and color.
- Rubber stamps are a great way to add letters, words, and pictures to your books. Some rubber stamps are designed to be stamped with black ink, and then colored in with pencils and markers.
- Paper hole punches are great for adding design elements to your books. You can use the punched out shapes as decorations.
- Great accents include glitter, stickers, charms, beads, buttons, jewels, and flat-backed glass marbles.

Lettering Your Books

Lettering can be added by hand with a marker, or you can purchase stick-on letters, use a stencil, or print out words and stories on a computer printer, cut them out, and glue them in place. It's fun to experiment with colored paper in your printer, but be sure to check the package to make sure the paper is okay to use in your machine.

Items for Binding

Bindings can be almost any kind of string, cord, ribbon, or just about any kind of wire. (If you don't have chenille stems or plastic-coated wire, trash bag twist-ties will work in a pinch!) Unusual items, like hair elastics, barrettes, binder clips and rings, or snaps can be used to hold the pages together. Take a trip to a hardware store, office supply store, or drugstore for inspirations for ideas to bind your own books.

Glues & Tapes

• White craft glue is my favorite — it holds fast and dries clear.
• Glue sticks are convenient and easy to use.
• Low-temp glue gun is best for a fast grab. Be careful not to touch the hot glue.
• Double-sided tape holds paper and craft foam flat without wrinkling.

Laminating Supplies

Laminating is a process that protects a surface by covering it with clear plastic adhesive film. You can buy laminating film that is acid-free in craft or scrapbook stores, or you can use clear self-adhesive paper as an easier (and cheaper) alternative. Or try wide *clear packing tape* for instant laminating.

Using the Patterns

1 Photocopy the pattern.

2 Cut it out along the solid lines.

3 Trace around the cut shape on the material that you're using for your project (paper, cardboard, felt, craft foam, etc.).

For a more permanent pattern, glue the copy to a piece of cardboard and cut out the shape. (This is called a template.) Use it to trace around and use as a pattern.

4 Easy Ways to Make a Basic Book

Here are ideas for four easy ways to bind your books. These books are decorated with small pieces of faux fur that was cut into shapes and glued in place with white glue. You can decorate your books in a number of ways – using paper, craft foam, felt, or fabric.

☀ 𝓑𝒶𝓈𝒾𝒸 Book #1
Start with a Notebook

SUPPLIES

- Spiral bound notebook, 5" x 3-1/2"

- Plush fur fabric (Choose a combination of spots and stripes.)

- White craft glue, Scissors, Pencil

1 Cut a piece of spotted fur fabric to cover the front of the notebook. Glue it to the front cover.

2 Using the pattern, cut the flower shape from striped fur fabric. Glue it on the cover.

3 Cut the flower center from a spotted print. Glue at the center of the petals. ❑

Look for patterns on page 17

☀ Basic Book #2

Staple a Book Together

1 Cut two pieces of cardboard, 5-1/4" × 3-1/4".

2 Staple the 3x5 cards together, three or four at a time, until they're all stapled in groups.

step 2

step 3

3 Tape the stapled groups together with double-sided tape.

4 Tape the front and back covers to the stack of cards along the edge. Use double-sided tape for this. The covers will be slightly bigger than the pages.

SUPPLIES

- Cardboard (for covers)
- 30 index (3"x5") cards for pages
- Plush fur fabric (for decorating)
- White craft glue
- Double-sided tape
- Stapler
- Scissors, Ruler, Pencil

5 Cut a piece of spotted fur fabric for the cover. Glue it on.

6 Using the pattern, cut the flower shape from striped fur fabric and the flower center from spotted fabric. Glue the flower on the cover. Glue the center onto the flower. ❏

step 6

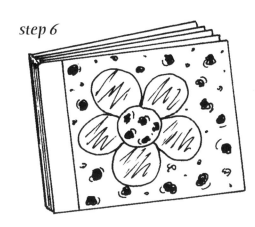

Look for patterns on page 17

☀ Book Idea #3
Hole Punch a Book

1 Cut two pieces of cardboard 3-1/4" × 5-1/4".

2 Punch three binding holes on one short side of each cardboard cover, lining up the holes so they match.

3 Punch three holes in each card, making sure the holes line up. You can punch two to three cards at a time.

step 2

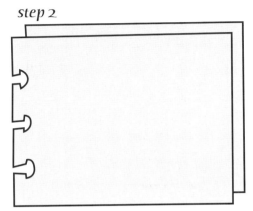

SUPPLIES

- Cardboard (for covers)
- 30 index (3"x5") cards (for pages)
- Plush fur fabric (Choose a combination of spots and stripes.)
- White craft glue
- Binding punch, guide, and 3 discs, 3/4"
- Scissors, Pencil, Ruler

4 Cut a piece of spotted fur fabric for the cover, being careful not to cover the punched holes. Glue it on.

5 Using the pattern, cut the flower shape from striped fur fabric and the flower center from spotted fabric. Glue the flower on the cover. Glue the center onto the flower.

6 Assemble the book. Insert three discs in the holes on the back cover, press the punched card pages on the discs, and press the front cover on the discs. ❏

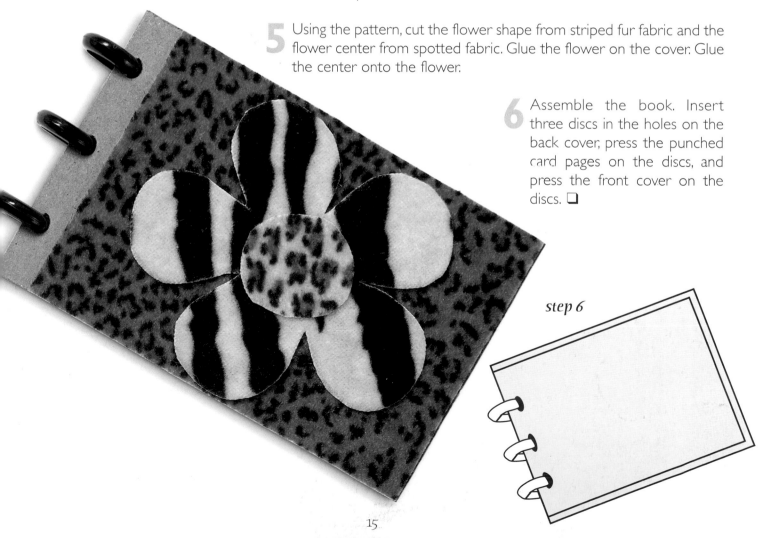

step 6

☀ Basic Book #4
Tie a Book Together

1 Cut two pieces of cardboard, 5-1/4" × 3-1/4".

2 Punch two holes along the short edge.

step 2

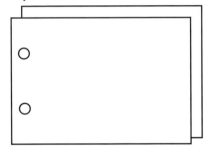

3 Line up the cards with the covers. Punch two holes in all the cards. You can punch two to three cards at a time.

step 3

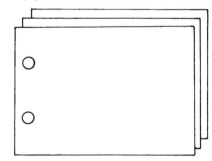

4 Cut a piece of spotted fur fabric for the cover, being careful not to cover the punched holes. Glue it on.

5 Using the pattern, cut the flower shape from striped fur fabric and the flower center from spotted fabric. Glue the flower on the cover. Glue the center onto the flower.

6 Thread the cord through the first hole, going from front to back. Leave a long tail on the front. Bring cord back to the front and down through the same hole again.

7 The end of the cord is now at the back. Take the cord down to the second hole and thread it up to the front of the book. Take the cord over the end of book and to back of hole.

8 Thread the cord through the bottom hole and up to the front again.

9 Tie the two ends of the cord in a bow or knot on the front cover. ❑

SUPPLIES
- Cardboard (for covers)
- 30 index (3"×5") cards for pages
- Plush fur fabric (Choose a combination of spots and stripes.)
- White craft glue
- 18" black cord or narrow black ribbon
- Hole punch
- Scissors, Pencil, Ruler

steps 6 & 7

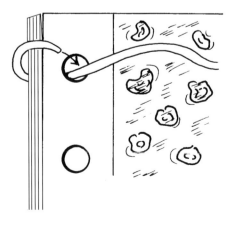

step 8

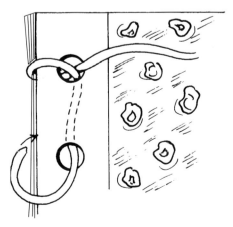

Flower
Petals

Flower
Center

Slipcovered Journals

You can make a plain book a special place to write or draw with slipcovers you make from fabric scraps, trims, and glue. Sew these book covers instead of gluing them if you're handy with a needle and thread or a sewing machine — just stitch along the edges.

SUPPLIES

- Purchased blank books, journals, or spiral bound notebooks
- Fabric or felt pieces
- Trims, buttons, silk flowers
- White craft glue
- Scissors, Ruler, Pencil

step 1

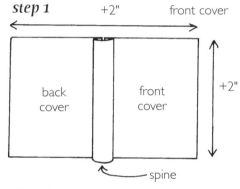

+2"   front cover

back cover

front cover

+2"

spine

If you're using a lightweight fabric that's easy to tear, you can get a nice fringed edge. Make a small cut, tear a straight line, and pull some threads away to make the fringe.

If you're using felt, cut it with scissors since the fabric won't tear.

1 Open the book, place it face down. Measure the width of the book, from one side to the other and across the spine. Add 2" to that measurement. Measure the height of the blank book. Add 2".

2 Cut the fabric or felt for the slipcover according to the measurements.

step 3

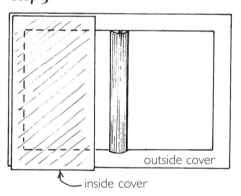

inside cover

outside cover

3 Cut or tear the two pieces of fabric for the inside of the cover. Make the two pieces the height of the outer slipcover and as wide as the cover of the blank book.

4 Sandwich the blank book covers between the outer slipcover piece and inside slipcover pieces. Glue the slipcover together around the edges.

5 Decorate with trims, flowers, and scraps of fabric. ❑

step 4

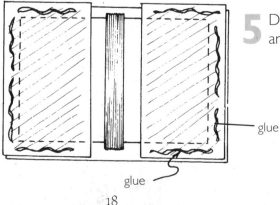

glue

glue

Friends Books

These personalized books make great party favors or gifts for favorite friends. They are easy – just decorate spiral-bound notepads you purchase at a store. After you decorate with big craft foam initials, tie on plastic bangles so the books can be worn as a bracelet.

Size: 3" x 5"

SUPPLIES

- Spiral bound notepads, 3" x 5"
- Craft foam – a variety of colors
- Plastic bangle bracelets and rings, one set for each notebook
- 1/4" wide ribbon, 10" for each book
- White glue, low temp hot glue gun, *or* craft foam glue
- Scissors, Pencil

1 Trace around the cover of the notebook on a piece of craft foam.

2 Cut out the foam.

3 Glue foam piece to the note-book cover.

4 Use the alphabet patterns given in this book to cut out your friends' initials from craft foam.

5 Glue a foam letter to the front cover of each book then decorate with small foam shapes in different colors.

6 Use the ribbon to tie a bracelet and ring to the spiral binding. ❑

step 1

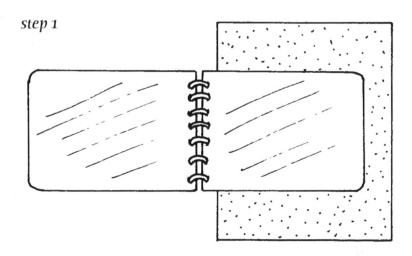

step 5

A B C D

E F Ç H I

J K L M

N O P Q

R S T
U V W
X Y Z

Alphabet Patterns

Birthday Books

A birthday book is a place to record the birthdays of your family members and friends. You can use them to keep track of other special events, too.

The two larger books each have 12 pages – one for each month of the year – so you can record the birthdays for each month on that month's page. The small book has 31 pages, one for each of the days of a month. In that book, you'd record the month and person's name on the correct date page.

The pages are made from tags from office supply stores. The covers, cut in the same shape as the tags, are decorated with a collage made of recycled birthday cards, scraps of wrapping paper, and stickers.

Month-by-Month Birthday Books

Cover size: 2-3/4" x 5"

Page size: 2-3/8" x 4-3/4"

SUPPLIES

- 2 tag-shaped pieces cut from small pieces of cardboard or cardstock (for the covers)
- 12 tags (for the pages)
- White glue, glue stick *or* double-sided tape
- Collage materials such as birthday cards, bits of wrapping paper or doilies, computer printouts
- Round stickers
- Binder rings or key rings
- Hole punch
- Marker (for lettering)
- Scissors, Pencil, Ruler

step 1

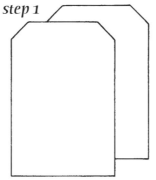

step 3

step 6

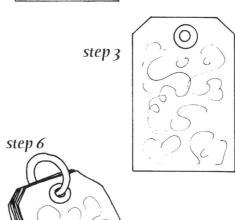

1 Cut 2 covers from cardstock, using the pattern provided.

2 Decorate the front cover with pieces cut from your favorite birthday cards. Add words cut from the printing inside the cards or words printed on your computer.

3 Put a round sticker on the front cover over the spot where the hole goes. Punch at the center of the sticker.

4 Punch a hole in the same spot on the back cover.

5 Write the name of each month on a tag or print out the names of the months on your computer printer, cut them out, and glue one on each page.

6 Thread the front cover, the 12 pages, and the back cover on a binder ring.

24

Day-by-Day Birthday Book

Size: 1-5/8" x 2-3/4"

SUPPLIES

- 32 tags (for the cover and pages)
- White glue *or* glue stick
- Collage materials (Stickers, birthday cards, gift wrap)
- Binder ring
- Hole punch
- Marker (for lettering)
- Scissors, Pencil, Ruler

1 Cut a piece of colored paper the same size and shape as a tag.

2 Glue to one tag to make the front cover.

3 Decorate the front cover with stickers or pieces cut from your favorite birthday cards.

4 Add words cut from the inside of the cards or printed from your computer.

5 Punch a hole in the cover over the hole in the tag.

6 Number the rest of the tags (1-31) for each day of the month.

7 Thread the front cover and the pages on a binder ring. ❏

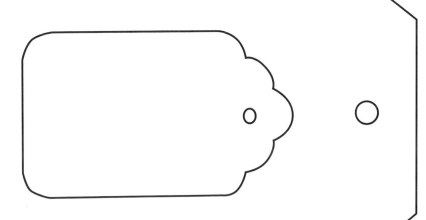

Keychain Books

Make these small accordion fold books to give as gifts or to hang on your backpack. Use them to collect autographs, phone numbers, or jokes. Or glue photos to the pages and take your friends and family with you wherever you go!

You could also hang one on a longer chain and wear it as a necklace!

Cover size:
2-1/4" square

Page size: 2" square

step 2

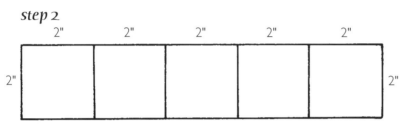

SUPPLIES

- Colored clear plastic file folders (for the covers)
- Colored cardstock or heavyweight paper (for the pages)
- Key chains
- Binder rings, key rings, or clips
- Small round hole punch
- Decorative hole punches (hearts, stars, etc.)
- Scissors, Pencil, Ruler

1 Cut a piece of cardstock 10" × 2".

2 Mark every 2" along the 10" side.

3 Fold like an accordion at every 2" mark.

step 3

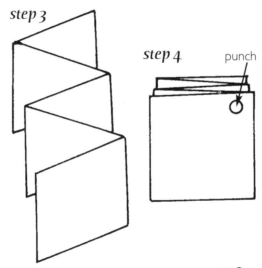

step 4

punch

4 Punch a hole in one corner of all the pages.

5 Cut a piece of file folder 2-1/4" × 4-1/2" for the cover. Fold it in half.

6 Punch a hole in the corner of the cover for the chain.

step 5, 6

fold

step 8, 9

7 With decorative hole punches, punch-out shapes on one side of the cover. The color of the pages will show through the punched holes.

8 Put the folded paper inside the plastic cover, lining up the holes. Insert the key chain through the holes.

9 Add a key ring, binder ring, or clip to the keychain. ❏

Almost ✪ Origami Books

Folded size: 2-1/2" square

Origami is the Japanese art of folding paper. This book has pages folded in a zig-zag pattern – that's not quite origami, but it is fun to do and a little challenging. Decorated cardboard covers laced with ribbon hold the pages together.

SUPPLIES

- Cardstock, cut into 12" squares (for pages)
- Thin cardboard (for cover)
- Double-sided tape
- White craft glue
- 1/2 yd. cord or thin ribbon
- Hole punch
- Decorations for the cover, such as flat-backed marbles, scraps of patterned paper, or handmade paper
- Scissors, Pencil, Ruler

1 Cut six strips of cardstock 2" wide. They can be all one color or two different colors.

2 Tape three pieces of one color end to end, overlapping them 1" inch. Repeat so you have two strips, 2" × 34".

3 Overlap the strips at corners and glue or tape them in place.

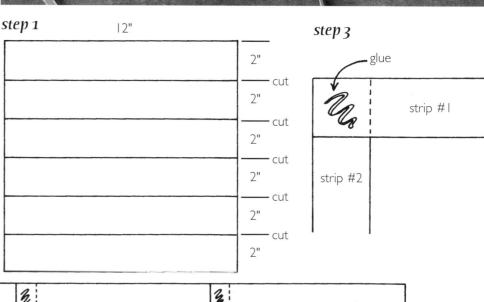

step 1   12"

2"
— cut
2"
— cut
2"
— cut
2"
— cut
2"
— cut
2"

step 3

glue

strip #1

strip #2

step 2

glue   glue

step 4

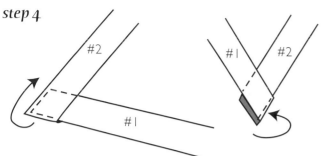

4 Fold each strip, overlapping them as you fold, till the strips are completely folded.

5 If you wish, gently pull the folded paper apart and mark the pages where you want to add photos or words. Unfold the book and write on or glue photos to those pages.

6 Glue or tape the last pages together on each end. Trim off any extra paper.

7 Cut two pieces of cardboard 2-1/2" square for the covers.

8 Glue the covers on the front and back of folded pages.

9 Decorate the cover.

Using Glass marbles: Glue patterned paper (such as a scrap of gift wrap) to the flat side of six clear flat-backed glass marbles, using white glue. (You'll be able to see the pattern through the marbles.) Let dry. Glue the marbles to the front cover. Let dry.

Using Handmade paper: Cut pieces of handmade paper to fit the front and back covers. Glue in place. Let dry.

10 Punch 2 holes on opposite sides of the front cover.

11 Glue the ribbon or cord to the bottom of the back cover. Bring the ribbon up the sides of the book and through the holes in the front cover. Tie the ribbon or cord in a bow. ❑

step 11

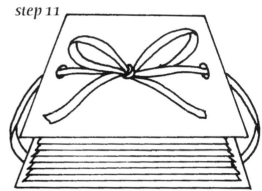

Funny Faces Photo Album

Make a personalized book for Mom or Dad and fill it with photos and keepsakes! Cutout comics and your own family's funny faces will make the cover extra silly. To make a more durable book, use color copies of comics and photos.

For the inside, find an inexpensive photo book with pages big enough to hold one picture. Don't worry about what the cover looks like – you're just going to use the inside pages.

Cover size: 5-1/2" x 6-3/8"

Page size: 5-1/4" x 6-1/8"

Note: The cover size is 1/4" larger in each dimension than the size of the pages. If your photo pages are a different size, adjust the size of the covers so the covers are a bit larger than the pages.

SUPPLIES
- Cardboard (for covers)
- Photo sleeve pages (from an inexpensive album)
- Comics
- Photos or color copies of photos
- Black paper
- Binding punch, guide, and 6 discs, 5/8"
- Glue
- Black pen and white paper
- *Optional:* Decorative hole punch
- Scissors, Ruler, Pencil

1 Cut the photo pages out of the album along the spine, making sure to cut them straight.

2 Cut two pieces of cardboard for the front and back covers.

3 Cut out some comics. Glue the pieces to the covers.

4 Cut a strip of black paper 1-3/4" x 6-1/8". Punch the edges of the paper to make it look like a film strip. Glue photos or photocopies of your photos to the black paper strip. Glue the black paper strip to front cover.

5 Print out the words "funny faces" on white paper or print them on your computer printer. Cut out and glue them to the front cover.

6 Using the binding punch and the guide, punch holes along one side of the front and back covers.

step 1

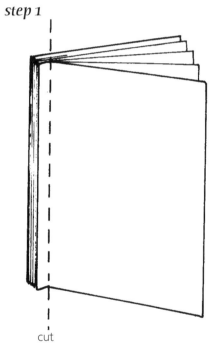

cut

step 6

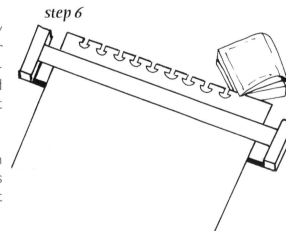

30

7 Punch holes along one side (the side you cut out of the album) of each photo sleeve page, using the guide to line up up the holes with the holes on the covers.

8 To bind the book, insert the discs in the holes on the back cover, press the inside pages on the discs, and press the front cover on the discs. ❑

step 8

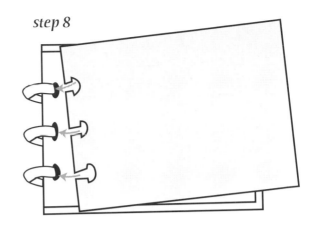

Pizza Box Scrapbook

Cover size: 9-1/4" square

Page size: 8-3/4" x 8-1/8"

Make your own scrapbook with a recycled pizza box cover. How do you get a pizza box? Order a small pizza, eat it, and then keep the box. Make sure it's clean and has no grease spots. Or ask your local pizza parlor to give you a clean box without pizza in it.

If you're planning to put photos in your scrapbook, you may want to choose acid free paper for the pages. Regular paper contains chemicals that can break down and harm your photos over time.

1 Cut off the top of the pizza box to make the front cover. Make it 9-1/4" or any size you wish.

2 Cut three pieces of colored posterboard the same size as the cover. *Tip:* Use the cutout pizza box top as a template and trace around it.

3 To round off the corners of the covers, place the coin on one corner. Trace around the edge of the coin with a pencil. Repeat on each corner. Cut on your pencil line.

4 Glue one piece of colored posterboard to the back of the pizza box top. It makes a colorful lining.

5 Glue the other two pieces of colored posterboard together, wrong sides together. This makes a stiffer back cover. Let dry.

step 3

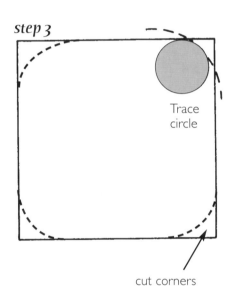

Trace circle

cut corners

6 Punch along one edge of each cover with the binding punch.

7 Cut out the pages for the inside of the book. They should be slightly smaller than the covers.

SUPPLIES

- Small pizza box (for front cover)
- Colored posterboard or cardstock (for back cover and front cover lining)
- Paper (for the pages)
- Binding punch, guide, and 8 discs, 3/4"
- Glue
- Coin or other round object, 1-3/4" diameter
- Scissors, Ruler, Pencil

Remember:

If you round the corners of the cover, the inside pages should be smaller.

step 8

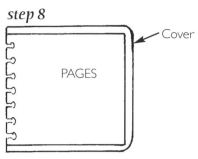

Cover

PAGES

8 Punch all the pages so the holes line up with the holes in the covers.

9 Assemble the book. Insert the discs in the back cover, press the inside pages on the discs, press the front cover on the discs. ❏

Cookie Cutter Books

You can purchase paper already cut into shapes in crafts stores like the Bunny Book or the Barefoot Book, or design your own by tracing around a cookie cutter. Add a set of covers, decorate them, and bind them together with some pretty hair elastics!

SUPPLIES

- Pre-cut paper shapes (25 pieces) *or* paper to cut into a shape using a cookie cutter for a template
- Hair elastics with plastic charms
- Plastic file folders (for front covers)
- Thin cardboard *or* cardstock (for back covers)
- Round hole punch
- Decorations for the front covers, like stickers or rhinestones
- Scissors, Pencil

step 1

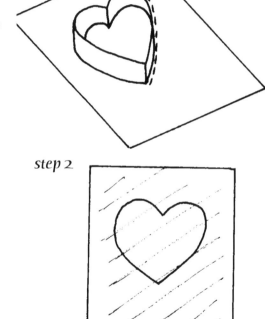

step 2

step 3

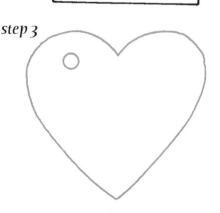

1 *If you're using a cookie cutter:* Using the cookie cutter as a template, trace around the shape on paper 25 times. Cut out the 25 shapes that will make the book pages.

2 *To make the front and back covers:* Place the cookie cutter or the shaped paper on the plastic file folder for front cover. Trace around it. Cut out the shape. Repeat this, using cardboard to cut out back cover.

3 Punch a hole in the same place on each page and on the covers.

4 Stack them together, lining up the holes, with the pages between the covers.

5 Insert a hair elastic, folded in half, through the hole. Slip the folded end of the elastic over the beaded end to secure.

6 Decorate the front cover any way you like. ❏

Snack Box Diaries

Recycle the cardboard boxes from your favorite snack boxes to make book covers. Oblong ones are the perfect size for a memo book, and you can use the folds from the boxes as folds on your covers. You could also use a tiny candy box to make a tiny sweet book!

Candy Box Book measures 6-3/4" x 4" with 5-1/2" x 3-1/2" pages
Popcorn Box Book measures 7" x 4-3/8" with 6-3/4" x 4" pages
Tiny Candy Box Book measures 2-1/2" x 1-1/2"

SUPPLIES
- Candy or other cardboard snack box (for cover)
- 7 sheets copy paper (for pages)
- 2 chenille stems
- 3 beads
- Hole punch
- Scissors, Ruler, Pencil

1 Flatten the box by opening both ends and taking the box apart on the glued seams.

2 Cut the box into two pieces so that the side of the box is along the top of the front cover and the other side is along the top of the back cover.

3 Punch three holes along one side of the front and back covers.

4 Cut paper for pages. Make 21 pages.

5 Punch holes in the pages that line up with the holes in the covers.

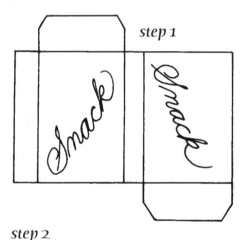
step 1

step 2

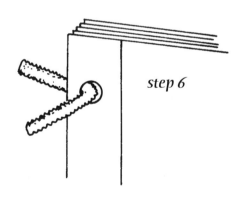
step 6

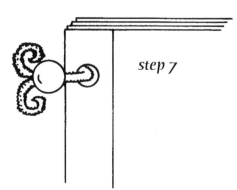
step 7

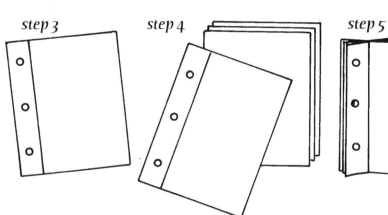
step 3   *step 4*   *step 5*

6 Cut chenille stems in half. Insert one piece of chenille stem through each hole.

7 Thread a bead on stem ends and curl the ends. ❏

Game Card Books

Here's an idea for using parts of a game that's missing too many pieces to play or a deck of cards where some of the cards got lost. Use the game cards or playing cards to make covers for tiny books. You'll need two cards for each book. You could also use the game's box to make the cover for a larger book.

SUPPLIES

- Playing cards or game cards (for covers)
- Paper, cardstock, or index cards (for pages)
- Binding punch, guide, and discs, 5/8" or 1/2" – 2 or 3 per book
- White glue *or* low temp glue gun and glue sticks
- *Optional:* Stick-on gems, wiggly eyes, sequin string

step 1

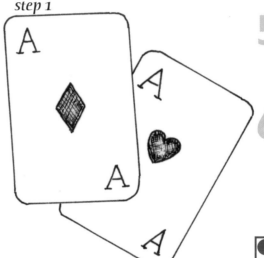

step 2

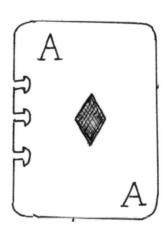

1 Choose one card for the front cover and one for the back cover.

2 Punch holes along one edge of each card.

3 Measure and cut paper for the inside pages of the book. (The pages should be slightly smaller than the covers.)

4 Punch the pages so the holes in the pages line up with the holes in the covers.

5 Put the book together. Insert discs in the back cover, press pages on the discs, and add the front cover.

6 Decorate the cover. Glue gems, sequins, or eyes with white glue or low temp glue gun. ❑

More Ideas

- If you use play money to make the covers, glue it to cardboard, then punch and insert the rings. Glitz up the cover with sequins!

- For a great gift, make each page of a book a coupon. Think of things you can do to help someone, like babysit or wash the car or vacuum. When the person who received the book redeems the coupons, you give the gift of your time.

Tiny Tote Books

Canvas Tote Book

*Canvas cover size (folded): 4" x 6"
(excluding handles)*

Book cover size: 3-1/4" x 5-1/8"

Page size: 3" x 5"

You never know when you'll need to write something down, so make a book with a strong canvas cover, grab the handles, and bring it wherever you go! You can purchase a small canvas bag at a crafts store. You could also use a small paper shopping bag with handles.

SUPPLIES

- Colored or patterned craft foam
- 25 Index cards, 3" x 5" size or paper cut to 3"x 5"
- Plastic-coated wire or cord
- Hole punch
- White glue or craft foam glue or low-temp glue gun and glue sticks
- Scissors, Pencil, Ruler

1 Turn the bag inside out. Cut off the sewn side seams, but leave the bottom seam attached.

step 1

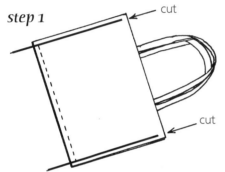

2 Pull a few threads from each cut edge to make fringe.

3 Dot the ends of the bottom seam with glue to keep the seam from coming apart.

step 3

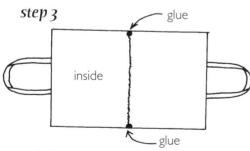

4 Punch two holes in the long side of the 3x5 cards.

5 Cut a piece of craft foam slightly larger than the cards for the front cover.

step 4

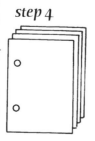

6 Punch two holes in the foam that line up with the holes in the cards.

7 Cut a 18" piece of wire or cord. Bind the cover and the inside pages and foam cover together with this. Thread the piece of wire through one of the holes from back up to front. Leave a tail about 4" long at back. Bring the wire over the edge of pages to the back. Thread back up through the hole to the front. Take the wire to the next hole and thread it to the back. Bring the wire from the back over the edge of the pages and back down the same hole. The end of the wire will be in back. Twist the two ends of the wire in back to secure. Trim ends.

8 Glue the back page of the book to the inside of the bag.

9 Cut 1" dots of craft foam and glue to outside of bag for decoration. ❑

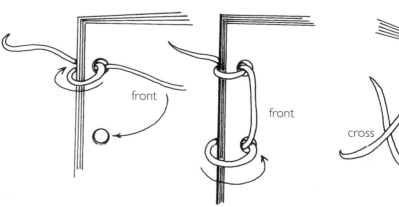

Paper Tote Book

Paper bag cover size (folded):
5" x 8" (excluding handles)

Page size: 4" x 6"

SUPPLIES

- Small kraft paper shopping bag with handles
- Blank paper (for pages)
- Thin cardboard
- Plastic-coated wire *or* cord
- 2 pre-cut cardboard shapes (from the scrapbooking section of a crafts store)
- Hole punch
- White glue *or* low-temp glue gun and glue sticks
- Scissors, Pencil, Ruler

1 Cut two pieces for the front and back by cutting the sides and the bottom off of the folded bag. You need two pieces, each 5-1/4" x 8", not including the handles.

2 Overlap the bottom edge of the front and back and glue together. Fold in half.

3 Cut paper to make pages.

4 Cut a piece of cardboard to the same size as the pages to make an inside back cover.

5 Punch two holes in the long sides of the pages and the cardboard.

6 Stack the pages on top of the cardboard "inside back cover" and bind together by threading with plastic-coated wire or narrow cord.

7 Glue the cardboard to the inside of the bag's back cover.

8 Decorate the front with precut corrugated cardboard shapes. ❏

Hand to Hand Autograph Books

Collecting autographs is a wonderful way to remember your friends. This is a fun project for a party — everyone will go home with a book.

Book with Clear Covers

The pages of this book are each a slightly different shape and size because a different person's hand was used as a template for each page. Get each friend to write a message on her hand page. Finally, bind them together into a nifty book.

SUPPLIES
- Clear plastic file folder (for covers)
- Multicolored paper or cardstock (for pages)

18-20 beads

- Hole punch
- Scissors, Ruler, Pencil

1 Have each of your friends place her hand on a piece of paper. Trace around the shape with a pencil. Be sure she includes part of her wrist. Cut out the shape. Make enough so each person has one of everybody's hand cutouts.

2 Ask everyone to sign their hand shapes and write a special message. Exchange them with each other so each person has one hand of her own and one hand from each of the others there.

3 Punch two holes in the wrist of each hand.

4 For each book, cut two pieces from a clear plastic file folder. Each should be large enough to cover the hands, and they should be the same size.

5 Line up the two covers with the hand pages and punch two holes in each cover that line up with the holes in the hands.

step 3

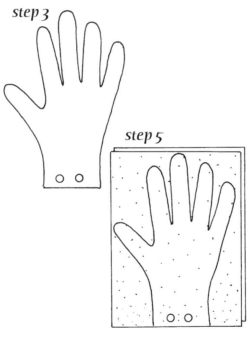

step 5

6 Insert a chenille stem back to front through one hole.

7 Place beads on the chenille stem to create a bracelet on the wrist.

8 Pass the end of the stem through the second hole to the back. Twist the ends of the chenille stem to secure.

9 Add more beads to each end of the chenille stem. Curl the ends of the stem to keep the beads from falling off. ❏

step 7

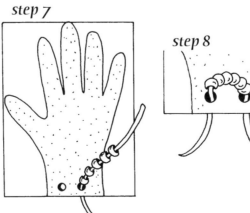

step 8

step 9

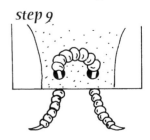

Book with Rectangular Pages

SUPPLIES

- Craft foam
- 8 sheets colored paper
- 8-10 beads
- 2 chenille stems
- Hole punch
- Scissors, Ruler, Pencil

1 Cut your hand shape out of craft foam. Punch two holes at the wrist.

2 Cut colored paper in rectangle shape to fit behind the hand shape.

3 Cut a piece of foam the same size of pages for the back cover.

4 Punch holes in the paper and the back cover that line up with the holes in the hand.

5 String five or more beads on a chenille stem. Slip it through the punched holes so it holds the book together and makes a bracelet on the hand.

6 String three beads on a piece of chenille stem. Loop it over the third finger on the hand to make a ring. ❑

Clear Cover Book:

Size: 7-3/4" x 5"

Pictured at bottom

Colored Cover:

Size: 7-3/4" x 5-3/8"

Pictured at top

Wish Journals

We all need a place to write down our special private wishes. This accordion-folded journal is a great place to keep track of dreams and wishes you never want to forget.

Handmade Paper Wish Journal

1 Cut a piece of handmade paper 7" x 36". Mark it every 3".

step 1

36"

7" | 3" | 3" | 3" | 3" | 3" | 3" | 3" | 3" | 3" | 3" | 3" | 3" |

SUPPLIES

- Handmade paper
- Off-white cardstock
- Scraps of black paper
- 1 yd. ribbon (for binding)
- Hole punch
- Permanent glue stick, white glue *or* double-stick tape
- Gold marker
- Black fine point marker
- Alphabet stencil with 7/8" letters
- Silver star stickers
- Scissors, Ruler, Pencil

2 Fold the paper on the marks (every 3") accordion style.

step 2

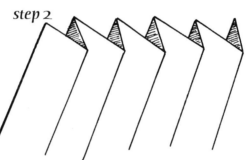

3 Cut 12 pieces of cardstock 6" x 2" – one for each panel of the accordion folds. These are for writing your wishes.

4 Glue or tape one piece of cardstock in the center of each page.

step 4

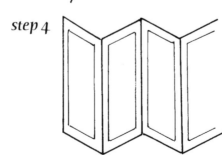

5 Fold up the book. Punch a hole in all the layers of the accordion folds on both long sides of the book.

step 5

6 Stencil the letters W-I-S-H with a gold marker on scraps of black paper. Cut out the letters and glue on the cover.

7 Write the word "journal" with a marker.

8 Decorate with a silver star sticker.

9 Cut two pieces of ribbon, each 18" long. Thread one ribbon through the holes on one side and tie in a bow. Repeat with the remaining piece of ribbon through the other set of holes.

Folded size: 4-1/2" x 6"

Unfolded size: 6" x 27"

Folded size: 7" x 3-3/8"

Unfolded size: 7" x 36"

Kraft Paper Wish Journal

You can make your book any size you wish. The book made from brown paper is 6" x 27" and is folded every 4-1/2." Make this the same way as the handmade paper journal. ❑

Sleepover Journals

Make these books for the guests at your next sleepover, or invite your friends to make their own during your party. You can record the secrets shared or recipes for snacks you ate or even paste in pictures of your pals in their PJs. And nobody has to worry about forgetting a toothbrush!

Large Book

Cover size: 7" x 6"
Page size: 6-1/12" x 5-1/2"

SUPPLIES

- Stiff felt fabric (for cover)
- 25 pom-poms, 1-1/2" (15 pink, 10 white)
- 2/3 yd. ribbon, 3/8" wide
- Paper (for pages)
- Toothbrush
- Hole punch
- White glue *or* low-temp glue gun and glue sticks
- Scissors, Ruler, Pencil

1. Cut the front and back covers from the felt. Punch two holes on one short side of each cover.

2. Cut paper for the pages. Make as many as you wish.

3. Punch holes in the pages along one side that line up with the holes in the covers.

4. Cut ribbon into two 12" pieces. Lace one ribbon piece through each set of holes. Tie each ribbon in a knot.

5. Place the toothbrush along the side where the holes are. Tie the ribbon in a bow around the toothbrush.

6. Glue five rows of five pom-poms each on the front cover, alternating colors. ❏

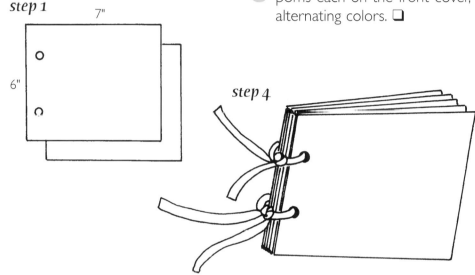

step 1

7"

6"

step 4

Small Book

Cover size: 2-3/4" x 2-3/4"
Page size: 2-1/2" x 2-1/2"

1. Cut 2 pieces of felt for the covers.

2. Cut 10 paper pages.

3. Punch two holes on one side of each cover.

4. Punch holes in the pages, lining up the holes with the holes in the covers.

5. Cut the chenille stem in half. Thread one piece through each of the holes. Twist to secure.

6. Place the toothbrush along the side of the book. Wrap the ends of the stems around the toothbrush. Curl the ends of the stems.

7. Glue the pom-poms on the front cover in a flower shape. ❏

SUPPLIES

- Stiff felt fabric
- 5 white pom-poms, 1"
- 1 blue pom-pom, 1/2"
- Paper (for pages)
- Toothbrush
- 1 chenille stem
- Hole punch
- White glue *or* low-temp glue gun and glue sticks
- Scissors, Ruler, Pencil

School Year Memory Books

Here's an idea that's easier than a scrapbook: Bind a memory book of readymade envelopes! Large envelopes have plenty of room for photos, programs, ticket stubs, hair ribbons – whatever you treasure, whatever you want to keep.

Use 10 envelopes (one for each month of the school year) or a few larger envelopes (one for each year of high school or middle school). Here are two options – one using manila envelopes, the other using transparent plastic ones.

Transparent Envelope Memory Book

SUPPLIES

- 4 transparent envelopes with string closure

- Binding punch, guide, and 3 discs, 1-1/4" diameter

- 1 yd. ribbon, 3" wide

- Stick-on letters

1 Punch three holes along the bottom edge of the envelopes using the punch and guide.

2 Insert discs to bind them together.

3 Add some stick-on letters to label each envelope.

4 Tie them together with a piece of ribbon. ❏

step 4

Manila Envelope Memory Book

SUPPLIES

- 10 manila envelopes, 10" × 13"
- Binding punch, guide, and 5 discs, 7/8"
- Colored posterboard or cardstock
- Colored paper
- Glue *or* double-stick tape
- Alphabet and decorative rubber stamps and stamp pad
- 2 Sticky dots
- Rickrack, ribbon, *or* cord
- Hole punch
- Scissors, Ruler, Pencil

1 Punch 5 holes along the bottom edge of 10 manila envelopes using the punch and guide.

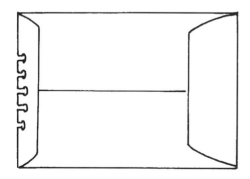

2 Cut a piece of cardboard the same size as the envelopes and punch to match the envelopes. This will be the back cover.

3 Insert discs in back cover, then press the envelopes onto the disks to bind them together.

4 Cut a piece of cardboard 6" × 13" with zig-zag edges. This is the front cover.

5 Punch one of the short edges of the front cover to match the envelopes.

6 Stamp words and decorative motifs on colored paper. Cut out the words and motifs.

7 Glue the words and decorative elements to the front cover.

8 Bind the front cover to the envelopes.

9 Place a sticky dot on the outside of the front and back covers.

10 Using a hole punch, punch a hole in the center of each sticky dot.

11 Lace with ribbon, rickrack, or cord through the holes and tie. ❑

Pop Art Sketchbooks

Large Book: 9" x 8"

If you think this looks like a big matchbook, you're right! I took the shape of a matchbook and enlarged it to create a sketchbook. The front cover is decorated with enlarged photocopies of common items and colored to look like pop art from the 1960s.

SUPPLIES

- Posterboard (for covers)
- Paper for inside pages, 8-1/2" x 14"
- 6 buttons (2 for each hole)
- 18" plastic coated wire (a 6" piece for each hole)
- Black and white copies of an ordinary item (I used a paperclip)
- Washable or watercolor markers
- Glue stick *or* double-stick tape
- Hole punch
- Scissors, Pencil, Ruler

1 Cut a piece of posterboard 9" x 19".

2 Score lines on the posterboard at 2-1/4", 10-1/4", and 12-1/4" from one short edge. Scoring makes it easy to fold. To score, run the back side (not the cutting edge) of a scissors on the posterboard along the edge of a ruler – you press a line, but you don't cut it.

3 Fold along the scored lines.

4 Fold up the bottom flap. Punch three holes across this flap, punching through the back of the posterboard.

5 Position the pages under the punched holes in the cover. Punch holes in the pages to match the holes in the cover.

6 Place a button over one of the holes on the back. Fold one piece of wire in half. Insert the ends through the holes in the button.

7 Push the ends of the wire through the hole on the back, the holes in the pages, and the hole in the front. Insert the ends of the wire through the holes in a second button. Twist wire to secure it and curl the ends. Repeat for the other holes.

8 Make Pop art to fit the cover. (See the box "Making Pop Art.")

9 Glue or tape your Pop art to the cover.

step 2

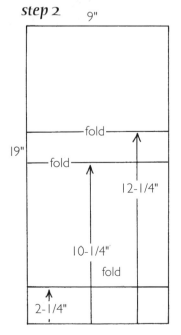

step 4

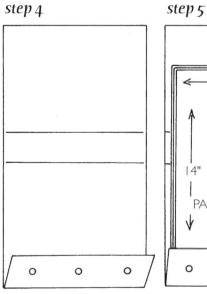

step 5

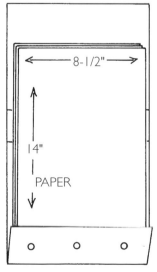

step 6

step 7

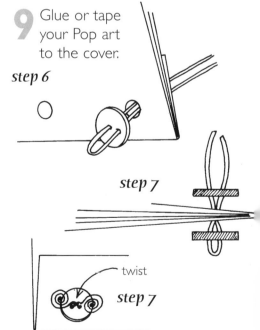

Small Book

Size: 5-1/2" square

SUPPLIES

- Posterboard (for cover)
- Paper for inside pages, 5" × 5"
- 4 buttons (2 for each hole)
- 12" plastic-coated wire (a 6" piece for each hole)
- Black and white copies of an ordinary item (I used a button.)
- Washable or watercolor markers
- Glue stick *or* double-stick tape
- Hole punch
- Scissors, Pencil, Ruler

1 Cut a piece of posterboard 5-1/2" × 11-1/2".

2 Score lines on the posterboard at 1-1/2", 6-1/2", and 7-1/2" from one short edge. Scoring cardboard makes it easy to fold. To score, run the back side of a scissors on the cardboard along the edge of a ruler – you press a line, but you don't cut it. Fold along the scored lines.

3 Fold the bottom flap up. Punch two holes in flap, punching through back cover.

4 Continue making this book the same way as the larger book. ❑

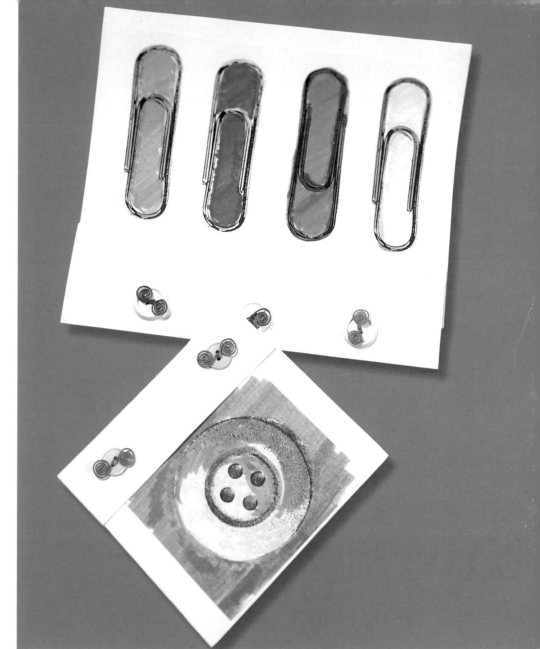

Making Pop Art

Andy Warhol, a famous artist in the 1960s, used mass production techniques – like photocopiers – to create works of art. His artwork now hangs in many museums. Here's a simple Pop art technique:

1. Choose something ordinary, like a button or a paperclip.

2. Enlarge it on a black and white photocopier.

3. Take the enlargement and enlarge it again. Keep enlarging till the image is the size you need to fit the cover of your book.

4. Color the copy with markers. (You don't have to be precise!) ❑

CD Holder Album

This is a great high-tech looking holder for anyone you know who loves music. I used black plastic needlepoint canvas for the cover, but it comes in other colors. It's easy to cut straight along the lines.

Cover size: 5-3/4" x 6"

Page size: 5-1/4" square

1 Cut the CD holder pages out of the book. Make sure you cut them out straight along the spine of the book.

2 Punch two holes in each page on the left edge. Make sure the holes are close to the top and bottom, so they don't interfere with the space where the CD goes.

3 Cut two pieces of plastic canvas 5-3/4" x 6" each for the covers. Punch two holes in each cover that line up with the holes in the CD pages.

4 Open the two binder rings. Place the CD pages inside the covers. Insert the rings through the holes to bind the covers and pages together.

5 Cut a circle out of silver cardboard to make a tag. Punch a hole in it. Label it, using a marker. Attach it to one of the rings with a keychain. ❑

SUPPLIES
- CD book with holder pages *or* about 20 individual CD holder pages
- Black plastic needlepoint canvas
- 2 binder rings, 1"
- Hole punch
- Silver cardboard (for a nametag)
- Keychain (to attach the nametag)
- Permanent fine tip marker (to label the tag)
- Scissors, Ruler, Pencil

step 1

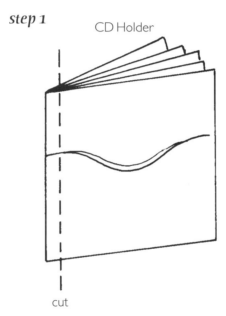

CD Holder

cut

step 2

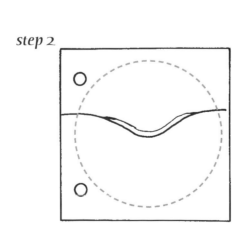

step 3

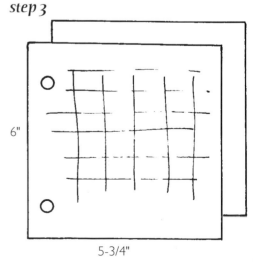

6"

5-3/4"

DAD's
CD's

Nature Journal

You can use this journal to write about a walk through the woods, a camping trip, or a vacation at the beach or use it as a place to save your collection of pressed flowers and feathers.

Cover size: 10-1/2" x 7"

Page size: 10-1/4" x 6-3/8"

Options: Glue an envelope inside the book to save your pressed flowers or bind a plastic slide holder into the book and fill each section with something you've gathered from the woods or the beach.

SUPPLIES
- Handmade paper (for covers)
- 2 twigs, 9" long
- Cord, *or* twine
- Paper (for pages)
- Colored paper (for leaf cutouts)
- Hole punch
- White glue
- Scissors, Ruler, Pencil
- *Optional:* Envelopes, plastic slide holder

1 Cut two pieces of handmade paper for the covers.

step 1

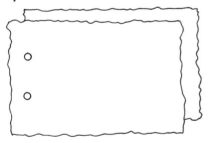

2 Punch two holes on one short edge.

3 Cut or tear paper for the pages.

4 Line up the cover with the pages. Punch two holes in each page.

5 Stack the covers with the pages inside so that the holes line up.

6 Wrap a piece of cord once around a twig. Place twig at back cover on edge with punched holes.

step 6

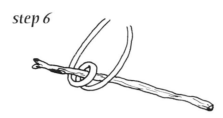

7 Bring both ends of cord up through one hole on the back cover. Tie cord ends around the second twig that you have placed on the front cover.

step 7

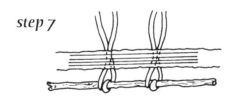

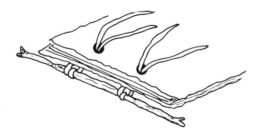

8 Repeat steps 7 and 8 for the second hole.

9 To decorate the cover, trace around some leaves on colored paper. Cut out the paper leaves and glue to cover. ❑

Collecting Nature
- To press flowers

In a book:
1. Cut the flowers close to the bottom of the bloom.
2. Line two pages of a heavy book (like a telephone book) with wax paper or blotting paper.
3. Carefully place your flowers on the page.
4. Close the book, and place under a stack of heavy books in a warm, dry place.

In a flower press:
Purchase a small flower press at a crafts store and follow the package instructions.

Handle pressed flowers carefully. To preserve them, place between two pieces of clear plastic adhesive laminate.

- To preserve the colors of fall leaves
1. Make color copies of them at the peak of their color.
2. Cut out the copies and glue them in your journal.

- To mount a feather on a page
1. Punch two tiny holes in a page.
2. Thread the feather through the holes.

Tic Tac Toe Book

The cover of this book is a game in itself. The inside pages can be used for hang-a-man or other word games.

Cover size: 8-1/2" square

Page size: 8" square

1 Cut four pieces of cardboard 8-1/2" square for the covers. Glue two pieces back to back. Glue the remaining two pieces together back to back. Let dry.

2 Punch along one edge of each cover with the binding punch.

3 Glue the plush felt piece to the front cover, lining up the edge of the felt with the right side of the cover, being careful not to cover the binding holes.

4 Cut four strips of white felt, 1/2" wide and 7-1/2" long. Glue them on the fuzzy felt cover.

5 Using the patterns provided, trace the X and O shapes on felt scraps. Trace enough to make 5 of each. Cut them out. Glue pieces together, placing the small dots on the larger circles and the small squares on the Xs.

6 Apply the "rough" (loop) side of the hook and loop dots to the backs of Xs and Os.

7 Cut paper for the pages.

step 1

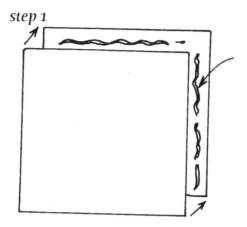

step 3

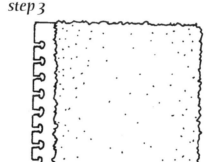

step 4

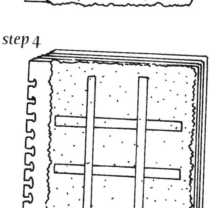

SUPPLIES

- 4 pieces lightweight cardboard or posterboard (for cover)

- Black plush felt fabric, 8" × 8-1/2"

- Scraps of felt, white and multiple colors (for the game pieces)

- 25 pieces of white paper (for pages)

- 10 sticky hook-and-loop fastener dots

- Binding punch, guide, and 8 discs, 5/8"

- White glue *or* low temp glue gun and glue sticks

- Ruler, Scissors, Pencil

8 Using the binding punch, punch holes along one side of the pages, lining up the holes with the holes in the covers.

9 Assemble the book. Insert the discs in the back cover, press the pages on the discs, then press the front cover on the discs to finish. ❏

Patterns

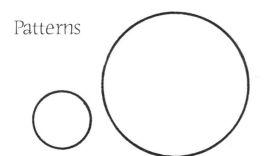
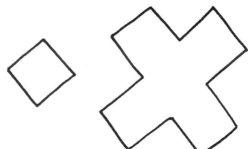

Vacation Journals

Years ago, before there were cameras and videos, people kept a journal to remember what they saw on a trip. This trip journal starts with a pocket folder and uses the bottom of your sneaker or shoe like a big stamp to decorate the cover. (You may want to make a practice print or two on scrap paper before you print on the cover of your book.) When you're finished printing, don't forget to wash your shoe!

You might like to bind some envelopes into the journal to hold the stuff you collect along the way, like ticket stubs, brochures, flyers, or menus. You can use readymade envelopes, or use the envelope pattern on page 65 to make your own with scrap paper.

I used rubber stamps to print the lettering for the title ("snaps scraps and souvenirs"), but you could hand write it or print it out on your computer printer. Shoelaces are used to hold the book together.

Cover size:
11-3/4" x 6"

Page size:
5-3/4" x 11"

SUPPLIES

- File folder with pockets in front and back (for the cover)

- Paper (for the pages)

- Sneaker

- Acrylic craft paint

- 1 pair shoelaces

- White glue *or* double-stick tape

- Paper towel

- Hole punch

- Pencil, Scissors, Ruler

- *Optional:* Envelopes, rubber stamps for title lettering and stamp pad

Variation

Postcards make great front and back covers for a journal. Simply cut as many paper pages as you like. Punch holes in the two postcard covers. Punch holes in the pages in the same places. Put all together and bind book with cord or binder rings.

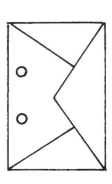

1 Measure 6" from the edge of both sides of the folder. Cut both sides (front and back) to create the front and back covers. Cut two strips 1" wide from the folder.

2 Glue the strips on the inside edge of the front and back covers to reinforce edge. Let dry.

3 Using the ruler, fold along the edge of the glued strip.

4 Punch four holes along the edge of the front and back covers.

5 Cut paper for the pages. Using the covers as a guide, punch four holes along the edges of the pages.

6 Fold a paper towel in quarters. Spread some acrylic craft paint on the paper towel to create a big stamp pad.

7 Press the painted towel on the bottom of your sneaker. The layer of paint on the bottom of the shoe should be pretty thick.

8 Carefully press the shoe on the front cover of the book to create the print. Let dry.

9 Cut two shoelaces in half. Thread one half through each of the four holes. Tie each in a knot, then in a bow. Knot the cut end of each to keep it from raveling.

10 Add the title to the book, using rubber stamps, handlettering, or words printed out on your computer.

Option: To add some envelope "pages," punch holes along one side of the envelope to line up with the holes in the pages. ❑

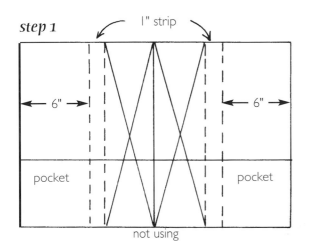

step 1

1" strip

6" 6"

pocket pocket

not using

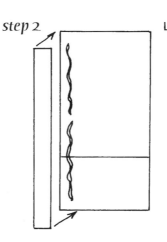

step 2 L

step 4

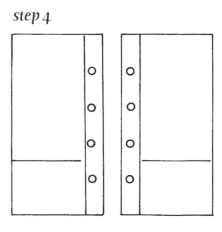

Locker Notebook

Cover size: 5" x 10"

Page size: 3" x 8"

A notebook is handy anywhere, but it's especially handy to have one inside your locker. This one has a magnet on the back, so it will stay put. When you run out of pages, it's simple to add more. The nifty loop at the bottom holds a pen. You can also cut out some shapes from colored magnet sheets in coordinating colors to use to hold notes and photos inside your locker.

SUPPLIES

- Craft foam
- Adhesive-backed sheet magnet, 5" x 8"
- Notebook paper
- 5-3/4" colored transparent plastic tubing, 1/2" diameter
- Stapler
- Low-temp glue gun and glue sticks *or* white glue *or* craft foam glue
- Scissors, Pencil, Ruler

1 Cut a piece of craft foam 5" x 10".

2 Cut 15-20 sheets of paper 3" x 8". Staple pages together at the top to make a pad.

3 Glue the top edge of the back piece of paper on the pad to the craft foam.

4 Cut a slit along the length of the plastic tubing. Slide the tubing over the top of the paper to cover the stapled edge.

5 Attach the magnet sheet to the back of the foam. Glue it if you are not using self-adhesive magnet sheets.

6 Cut a piece of foam 2" x 3" for the pen holder. Place around the bottom of the large piece of craft foam, making a loop for a pen holder. Glue it in place. ❑

step 1

10"

5"

step 2

3"

8"

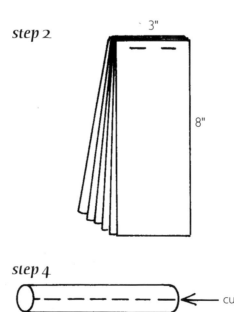

step 4

push

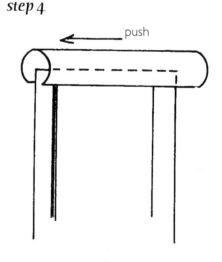

step 4

cut

Carry-All Book

Need a book on the go? How about this one? The tab keeps it closed and secure, and the built-in handles make it easy to carry. I used colored paper to make the pages, but you could use sketch paper instead for a carryall sketch book.

Cover size: 8-1/2" x 9"

Page size: 5-1/2" x 8-1/2"

SUPPLIES

- 2 sheets of craft foam (for the covers)
- Scraps of craft foam (for the fringe and tab)
- 8-1/2" x 11" colored paper (for pages)
- 5 large pony beads
- Sticky hook-and-loop dot
- 1/4" round hole punch
- Thick white glue, craft foam glue, or low-temp glue gun
- Scissors, Ruler, Pencil

step 1

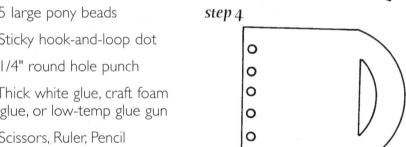

step 4

1 Make a copy of the pattern for covers. Cut it out.

2 Position the cover pattern on one piece of craft foam. Trace around it. Repeat with the other piece of craft foam. Cut out the covers.

3 Using the pattern, trace the tab on a scrap of foam. Cut it out.

4 Punch five holes along one edge of each cover, using the pattern as a guide.

5 Fold 10 to 12 sheets of 8-1/2" x 11" paper in half. Using the pattern as a guide for where to place the holes, punch five holes along the folded edge, working two sheets at a time.

6 Stack the covers with the pages in between them, lining up the punched holes.

7 Cut five strips of craft foam, each 1/8" wide and 6" long. Thread one strip through each hole, working from the back cover through the inside pages to the front cover. Slip a bead over the ends of the strips and slide the bead toward the cover.

8 Glue the end of the tab on the back cover. Glue one side of the hook-and-loop dot on the underside of the rounded end of the tab. Glue the other side of the dot on the front cover. ❏

step 7

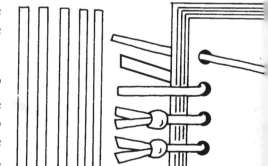

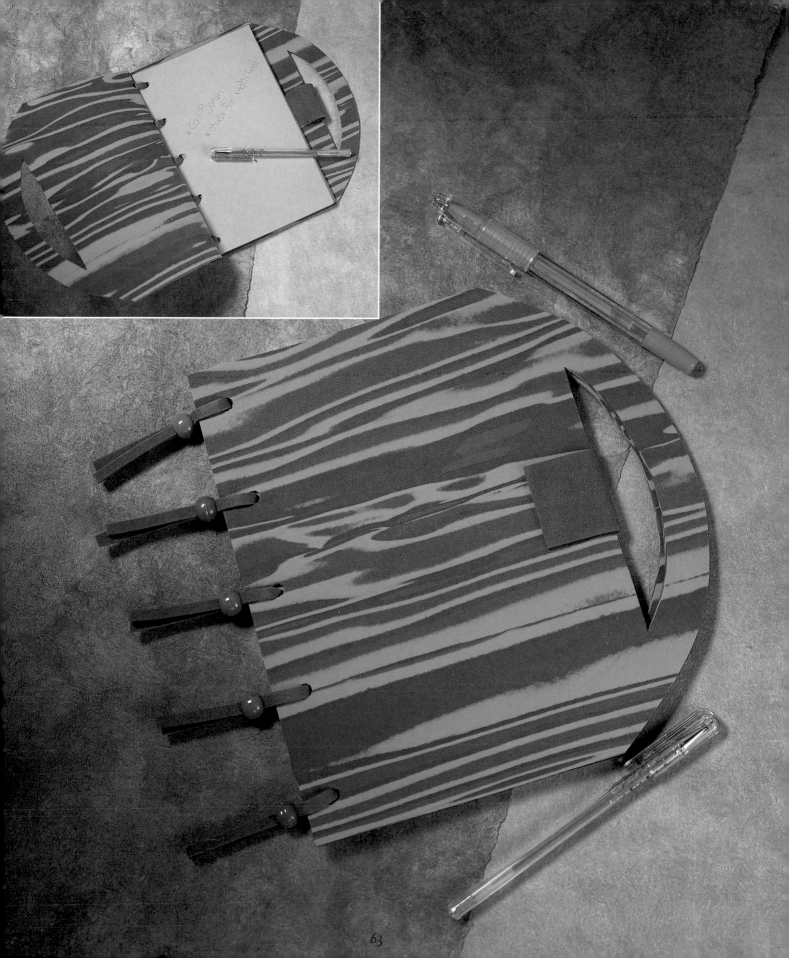

Carryall Book Pattern

Enlarage @120% for actual size

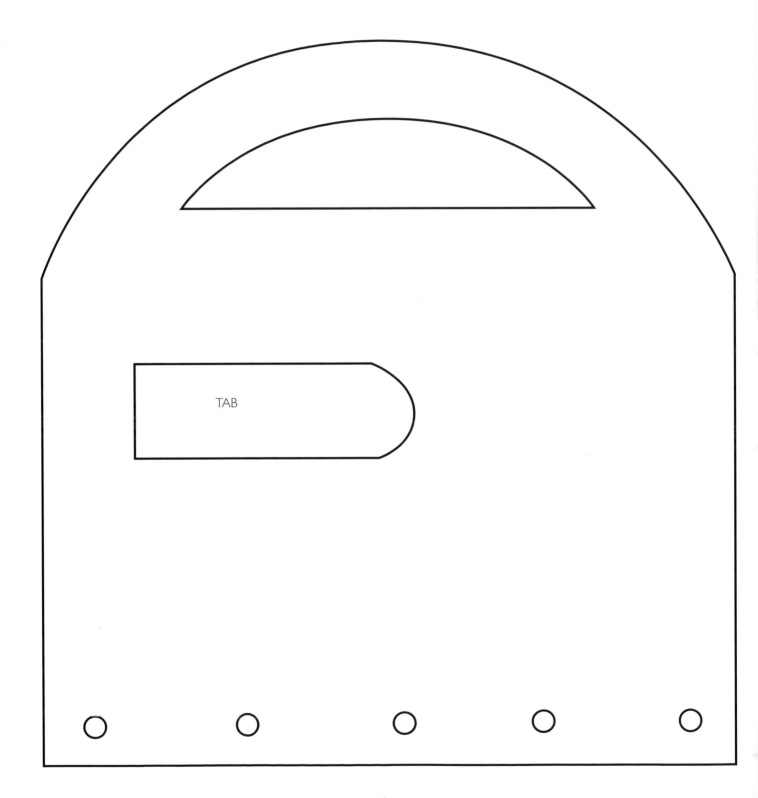

TAB

Envelope Diary Patterns

(See page 66 for instructions.)

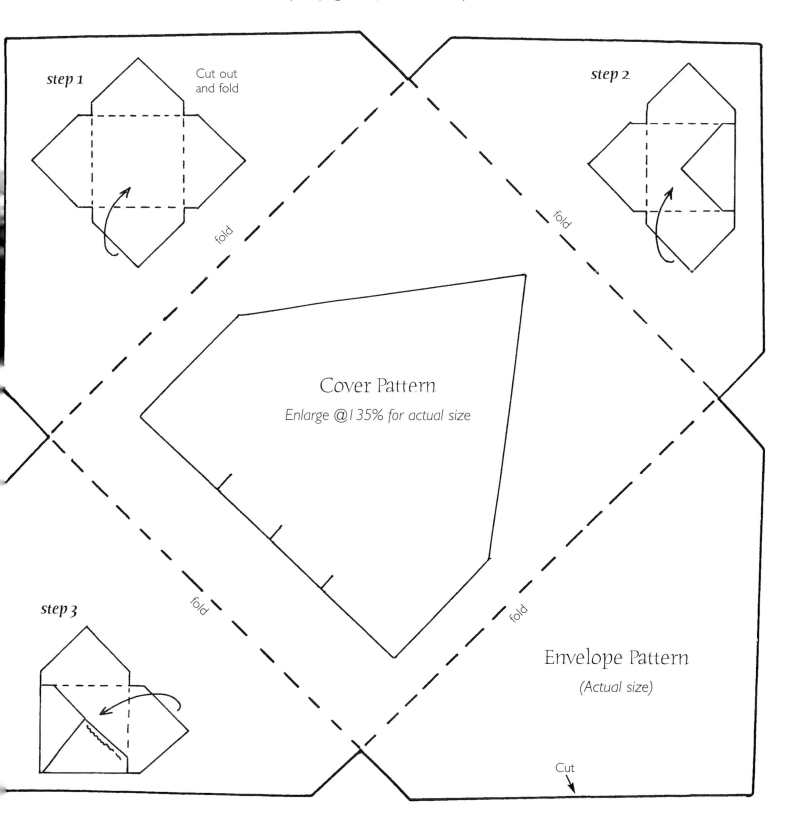

step 1

Cut out
and fold

fold

step 2

fold

Cover Pattern

Enlarge @135% for actual size

step 3

fold

fold

Envelope Pattern

(Actual size)

Cut

Envelope Diaries

You can make an envelope book in minutes with readymade envelopes, or — if you have more time — use the pattern on page 65 to make one-of-a-kind envelopes out of scrap paper or pages from your favorite magazine. Use the envelopes to collect letters, special notes, or secrets — you decide.

Handmade Envelope Book

Size: 5-1/4" x 4-3/4"

SUPPLIES
- Paper for making envelopes (I used pages cut from magazines.)
- Piece of a clear plastic file folder (for front cover)
- Cardstock or posterboard (for the back cover)
- Binding punch, guide, and 3 discs, 3/4"
- 10" of grosgrain ribbon, 3/8" wide
- Hole punch
- Glue stick or double-sided tape
- Fine tip marker (for labeling)
- Pencil, Scissors, Ruler

1 Using the envelope pattern on page 65, make 8 to 10 envelopes.

2 Cut a piece of cardboard the same size as the envelopes for the back cover. Punch a hole at the center point on the right edge of back cover.

3 Using the pattern provided on page 65, cut a piece of clear file folder for the front cover. Punch a hole in the point of front cover.

4 Choose a title and hand write it with a marker on a piece of paper, or print on your computer. Cut out the words and glue to the front cover.

5 Punch the left edges of back cover, the envelopes, and the front cover for binding.

6 Assemble the book. Insert three discs in the back cover, press the envelopes on the discs, and press the front cover on the discs.

7 Thread the ribbon through the two punched holes on the right edges of the covers and tie. ❏

Oblong Envelope Book

Size: 9-5/8" x 4-1/2"

SUPPLIES
- 8-10 business-size envelopes (for pages)
- Binding punch, guide, and 3 discs, 3/4"
- Cardstock or posterboard (for covers)
- Wrapping paper (for decorating the cover)
- 1/2 yd. ribbon
- Glue stick or double-sided tape
- Computer-printed lettering *or* fine tip marker (for labeling)
- Pencil, Scissors, Ruler

1 Cut two pieces of cardstock or posterboard the same size as the envelopes.

2 Glue wrapping paper to one piece to make the front cover.

3 Choose a title (this one is "gabbing girlfriends"). Print it out on your computer or hand write it with a marker on a piece of paper. Cut out the words and glue to the front cover.

step 2

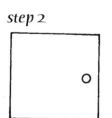

step 3

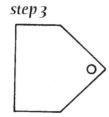

step 1

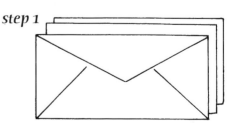

Tiny Envelope Book

Size: 3-1/2" x 2-1/4"

This was simply made by binding together several tiny manila envelopes. The first envelope is decorated.

This handmade envelope book has a clear plastic cover so you can see the neat envelopes made from magazine pages.

4 Punch the short edge of the back cover, centering the holes. Punch the envelopes, lining up the holes in them with the holes in the back cover. Punch the front cover to match.

5 Assemble the book. Insert three discs in the back cover, press the envelopes on the discs, and press the front cover on the discs.

6 Tie the ribbon around the book. ❑

step 2

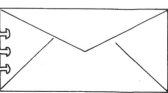

Bottle Cap Notebooks

Size: 3-1/2" x 4-1/4"

SUPPLIES

- Small ruled notebooks (3-1/2" x 4-1/4")
- Solid color paper (for covers)
- Sticky dots or stickers
- Bottle caps *or* jar lids
- Color copies of photos
- Circle template
- White glue
- Scissors, Pencil, Ruler
- *Optional:* Ribbons or cords

Frame your best friends' photos in bottle caps and glue them to the cover of a small notebook to carry with you for special notes, autographs, or phone numbers. You can find these small notebooks in stationery and discount stores. I decorated them with sticky dots and stickers, but you could also use rubber stamps or markers. Make color copies of your photos to preserve the originals, and use the copies to make your book.

1 Cut colored paper the same size as front cover and back cover. Glue piece to the covers of notebook.

step 1

2 Decorate the cover with sticky dots.

step 2

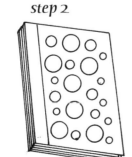

3 Choose a circle template that will fit inside the bottle caps or jar lids you've chosen. Use the template to cut out the photos. Glue the round photos inside the bottle caps or lids.

4 Glue the bottle caps or lids to the covers.

5 *Option:* Tape or glue ribbon or cord to the back cover and wrap and tie the books closed.

Scroll Happiness Journal

Size: 3-1/2" x 4-1/4"

SUPPLIES

- Card stock or heavy paper, 8-1/2" wide by 18" to 24" long (or length of your choice) – heavy wrapping paper works great.

- Chopsticks or wooden dowels

- Cord, shoelace, or ribbon to tie scroll, 30"

- Alphabet beads to spell a name or "happiness journal"

- Double stick tape

- Scissors, pencil, ruler

When you keep a list of the things that make you happy – you will be amazed at how many there are. Make a long scroll and use it every day to write down two or three things that make you happy or thankful. Pretty soon you'll have a list full of happy thoughts.

1 Place the 8-1/2" x 24" piece of paper for your scroll flat in front of you.

2 Lay two strips of double stick tape, side-by-side, along one short edge of the paper.

3 Wrap the taped edge of the paper around a dowel or chopstick. Make sure it holds.

4 Do the same thing on the other side of the paper.

5 Roll both ends of the scroll to the center, rolling the paper around the dowel.

6 Turn the scroll over. Tape or glue the center of your cord to the center of the back of the scroll.

7 Wrap the cord around the scroll and tie it in a bow or knot at the front of scroll.

8 String the alphabet beads onto the ends of the cord and knot the ends to keep the beads on. ❑

Pet Books

Here's a pet you don't have to feed, walk, or take to the vet. For the cover, use plush and fuzzy fabrics (available at crafts stores) or rescue pieces from a worn-out stuffed animal. Use pom-poms and felt to create happy or scary faces, or add sequins, gems, and feathers to create a glam animal face.

Large Book

Cover size: 8-1/2" x 6"

Page size: 8-1/4" x 5-5/8"

1 Measure and cut two pieces of posterboard for the covers.

2 Punch 6 holes with the binding punch along one edge of each cover.

3 Cut a piece of plush for the front cover (8" x 6"). Here's a tip for cutting plush fabric: Cut it from the back (non-furry) side. If possible, take the fabric outside to cut it to keep the plush hairs from getting everywhere!

4 Glue the plush piece to the cover, being careful not to cover the holes. Let the glue dry.

5 Glue on pom-pom eyes and plush eyebrows to create a pet face. Cut felt circles to add to the eyes and glue in place. (You can use craft glue for this, but a glue gun is faster.)

6 Cut paper for the pages. Punch one edge of the pages to match the holes in the cover.

step 1

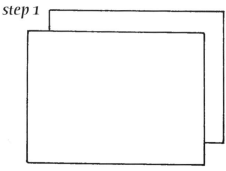

step 4

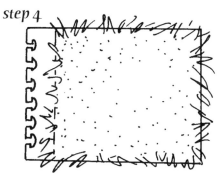

step 5

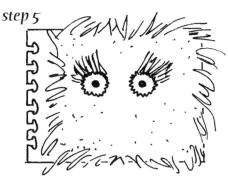

7 Assemble the book. Insert discs in the back cover, press pages on the discs, and press the front cover on the discs.

SUPPLIES

- Posterboard or lightweight cardboard (for covers)
- Paper (for pages)
- Plush fabric piece, at least 8" x 6" for the front cover plus some scraps in different colors
- 2 pom-poms, 1"
- Black felt scrap
- Binding punch, guide, and 6 discs, 1" diameter
- White glue *or* low temp glue gun and glue sticks
- Scissors, Pencil, Ruler

Small Book

Cover size: 5-3/4" x 4-1/2"

Page size: 5-3/8" x 4-1/4"

Make this the same way as the large book using these measurements. ❑

Necklace Diaries

These tiny books are fast and fun to make – you only need scraps of paper and some jazzy accents like appliques, charms, jump rings, clips, beads, spangles, or rubber stamps and ink. You can find jump rings, charms, and chains at crafts or bead stores or use parts from old costume jewelry. The books can be used for bracelets, too. Each one has 12 to 15 pages.

Clip Book

SUPPLIES

- Colored paper (for pages)
- Paper scraps (for decorations)
- Decorative hole punches
- Stapler
- Hanging plastic clip
- Ball keychain
- Glue
- Scissors, Ruler, Pencil

1 Cut paper for the pages 1-1/2" x 2".

2 Staple the pages on the top.

3 Punch decorative shapes from paper scraps or cut your own paper shapes with a scissors. Glue the shapes to the cover.

4 Clip the hanging plastic clip over the stapled side of paper.

5 Loop a ball chain through the hole in the clip. Add a touch of glue to the clip to keep it attached to the paper. ❏

step 1

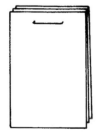

step 4

Personalized Bracelet Book

SUPPLIES

- Colored paper (for cover and pages)
- 15" cord
- Rubber stamp and inkpad
- Stapler
- Hole punch
- Spiral bracelet key ring
- Scissors, Ruler, Pencil

1 Cut paper for the pages 2" x 4".

2 Fold each in half.

3 Stack all the pages together and staple at the center of the fold.

Personalized Bracelet Book

4 Punch one hole in all the pages below the staple.

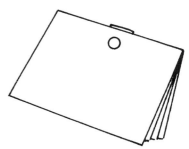

5 Decorate the cover with paper scraps and a rubber stamped name.

6 Fold the cord in half. Tie a small loop in the folded end. Thread the cord through the punched hole, then wrap and tie it around the book.

7 Attach the loop to the key ring. ❑

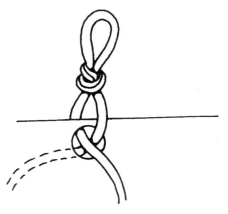

Butterfly Book

Pictured on page 73

SUPPLIES

- Paper in two colors (for pages)
- 1-1/2 yd. cord
- 2 beads
- Hole punch
- Sparkly applique
- Glue
- Scissors, Ruler, Pencil

1 Cut paper 1-3/4" × 2-1/4" for the pages.

2 Punch two small holes in the top of each page.

3 Cut two pieces of cord, each 24" long.

4 Thread one piece through each hole. Add a bead. Tie a knot above the bead. Knot cord ends together.

5 Glue a sparkly applique to the front. ❏

step 4

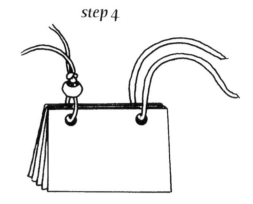

Charmed Book

Pictured top right on page 75

SUPPLIES

- Silver cardboard (for covers)
- Colored paper (for pages)
- Round hole punch
- Flower hole punch (large enough to loop cord through)
- 3/4 yd. black cord
- Jump ring
- Small silver or pewter charm
- Scissors, Ruler, Pencil

1 Cut paper for pages 1" × 2".

2 Cut a piece of silver cardboard slightly longer and wider for the back cover.

3 Cut a smaller square for the front cover.

4 Use the flower punch to punch front cover, each page, and the back cover – making sure holes are in the same place on each. Stack up the pages and the covers.

5 Loop the cord through the holes.

6 Punch a small round hole at the bottom of the back cover. Attach a charm with a jump ring. ❏

Front cover

Pages

Back cover

Spangled Book

SUPPLIES

- Clear 3-D plastic (for cover)
- White paper (for pages)
- 12 jump rings, 3/8"
- 6 silver spangles, 3/4
- 24" clear plastic cord with silver glitter
- Small round hole punch
- Scissors, Ruler, Pencil

1 Cut paper for the pages 1-1/2" × 2".

2 Cut a piece of 3-D plastic the same size for the front cover.

3 Cut a piece of 3-D plastic 1-7/8" × 1-1/2" for the back cover.

4 Punch six evenly spaced holes across one long edge of both covers and the pages, lining up the holes. Punch six holes along the bottom edge of the back cover.

5 Bind the top holes with large jump rings.

6 Add jump rings with spangles to the bottom edge of back cover.

7 Thread cord through the top rings and knot the ends together. ❏

Then and Now Photo Album

Cover size: 6" x 5"

Page size: 5-3/4" x 4-3/4"

If you're lucky enough to have grandparents, or great aunts and uncles around, then you know about the special stories they have to tell. Use this book to gather photos and souvenirs to remember your grandparents' lives, or give the book to them and ask them to fill in the pages with their memories for you.

1 Measure and cut a piece of cardboard 18" × 5". Score every 6".

18" — 6" — 6" — 6" — 5"

↑ score   ↑ score

2 Fold in a Z-shape.

score

3 Score a line 1" in from the fold on the front and back covers.

score

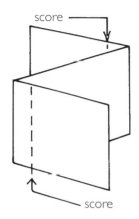

4 Punch two holes along each fold.

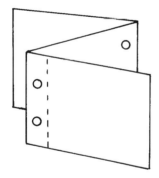

5 Cut 24 pieces of paper for the pages, 4-3/4" × 5-3/4".

6 Punch two holes in each sheet that line up with the holes in the covers.

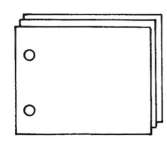

7 Place half the pages inside one fold of the cover and tie a potholder loop, cord, or ribbon through each hole to bind the book at the fold. Repeat with the remaining pages in the other fold.

8 Trim photocopied photos and insert in the badge holders. *Option:* Place the photos between two pieces of laminating film.

9 Punch holes in all four corners of the badge covers (or laminated photos).

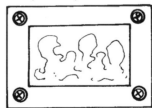

10 Position one badge holder on the front cover and mark where the holes are. Place the other badge holder on the back cover and mark the holes. Punch holes at the marks. Snap in snaps through the holes to attach the badge holders to the covers.

11 Write words like "Then" and "Now" on the badge holders with a paint marker. (Be careful! Paint markers are permanent.) ❏

SUPPLIES

- Black posterboard or lightweight cardboard (for covers)
- Paper (for pages)
- 2 badge holders *or* laminating film (to hold the photos)
- 2 photocopies of photos (one recent, one older)
- 4 potholder loops *or* 3/4 yd. cord or ribbon (for binding)
- 8 snaps (size no. 1 or larger)
- Paint marker
- Hole punch
- Scissors, Ruler, Pencil

Scoring

Scoring makes stiff paper and cardboard easy to fold. To score, run the back side of a scissors (not the sharpened blades) on the cardboard along the edge of a ruler — pressing a line, but not cutting it. Fold along the score. ❏

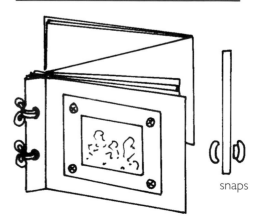

snaps

Hanging Memo Book

Make this handy memo book to hang on your bedroom door, near the phone, or anywhere someone may need to take a note. This book is made in folios. A folio is a folded piece of paper that makes four pages. For this book, four folios are stapled together to create a 16-page signature (a group of pages bound together). Most traditional books are made up of several signatures bound together with glue and/or stitching.

The signatures of this book are held together with a bulldog clip, which has a hole for hanging. As the pages are used and torn off, they can be replaced. If you make it as a gift, be sure to make additional signatures to go along with it as replacement pages. The cork pad on the bottom can be used to post notes or messages.

SUPPLIES

- Silver posterboard (for backing)
- Copy paper (for pages)
- Bulldog clip, 3" wide
- 2-3 cork shapes or coasters, 3-3/4" diameter
- Stapler
- White craft glue
- A few pushpins or decorative tacks
- *Optional:* Decorative scissors
- Scissors, Ruler, Pencil

1 Cut two pieces of silver cardboard 4" x 9-1/2". Glue them together, silver sides out.

2 Stack the cork shapes to make a thickness of about 1/2". It needs to be thick enough to hold a tack. Glue the cork shapes together. Let glue dry.

3 Make the page signatures. Cut the paper 3" x 11". Place four sheets together. Fold in half. Staple at the top. (Make at least four.)

4 Stack the signatures on top of the cardboard backboard with the folded edges of the signatures lined up along the top of the backboard. Clip them together with the bulldog clip.

5 Glue the stacked cork shapes to the bottom of the silver cardboard.

6 Insert the pushpins or tacks in the cork. ❑

step 1

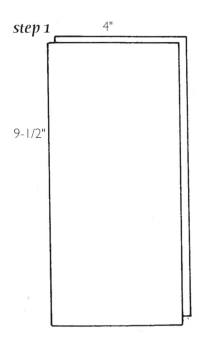

4"

9-1/2"

step 3

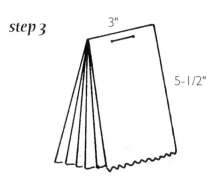

3"

5-1/2"

Option: Cut the bottom edge of some or all the sheets with decorative scissors.

Tie-dyed Dream Journal

Size: 8-1/2" square

Dreams are important – not just the ones you have at night, but your daydreams, too. To make sure you don't forget them, record your dreams in a groovy journal. Making the tie-dyed paper for the cover is easy but messy, so use a work surface that can get wet and is disposable or easy to clean.

SUPPLIES

for the Tie-dyed Paper:

- White paper towels
- Rubber bands
- Watercolor (or washable) markers
- Water

for the Book:

- Lightweight cardboard or posterboard (for the covers)
- Paper (for pages)
- Metallic cord
- 4 feathers
- 2 beads
- Glue stick
- Hole punch
- Silver glitter glue
- Scissors, Pencil, Ruler
- Small plate or other round shape (to use as a template)

Make the tie-dyed paper:

1 Pull the paper towel to a point at the center. Wrap the end with a rubber band. Wrap a couple more rubber bands along the gathered towel.

2 Make stripes with the water-color markers around the gathered towel near the rubber bands.

3 Take another paper towel, dip it in water, and squeeze most of the water out. Press the damp towel around the stripes until the colors start to bleed.

4 Before the colors bleed so much that they completely blend together, cut off the rubber bands with a scissors. Lay the tie-dyed towel flat to dry on a surface covered with paper. Let dry completely.

5 Press the tie-dyed towel with a cool iron between two pieces of cloth to make it flat.

Assemble the book:

6 Cut two posterboard pieces for front and back covers, each 8-1/2" square.

7 Glue the tie-dyed paper towel to front cover. *Don't use* white craft glue – it will make the tie-dyed colors run and bleed!

8 Place a small plate or other round shape (mine had a diameter of 8-1/4") on the cover with the tie-dyed towel glued on. Trace around it and cut out the circle. Trim off a little (about 1/4") on one side for binding.

9 Cut the pages, each to 8-1/4" square.

10 Punch two holes in the front cover. Then punch the pages and the back cover, lining up the holes with the holes in the front cover.

step 1

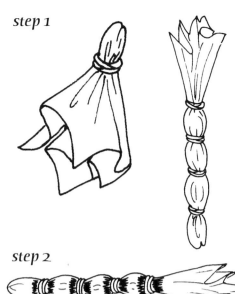

step 2

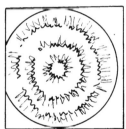

step 8

step 10

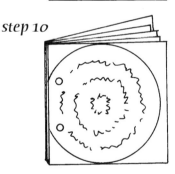

11 Tie with metallic cord to bind.

12 Decorate the ends of the cord with beads and feathers. Slip a bead over the end of the cord, glue feathers to the cord, slide a bead down over feathers, and glue in place.

13 Write "DREAM" with glitter glue on the front cover. ❏

Summer Diaries

Larger Book

Cover size: *5-3/4" x 8-3/4"*

Page size: *5-1/2" x 8-1/2"*

SUPPLIES

- Vinyl fabric
- 12 sheets white or colored copier paper, 8-1/2" x 11"
- 3 small barrettes or clips
- 1/4" round hole punch
- Scissors, Ruler, Pencil

They're lightweight, cool, and you can wipe them clean with a damp cloth! Perfect for taking to the beach. The covers are cut from vinyl tablecloth material (an old shower curtain or plastic tote bag would work as well), and the books are bound with little barrettes or clips. If you're in a glitzy mood, you could glue on some sequins or plastic gems.

1 Fold the 12 pieces of 8-1/2" x 11" paper in half.

2 Punch three holes along the folded edge of one sheet about 1/4" from the edge. Using this sheet as your guide, punch three holes in the rest of the sheets.

3 Measure and cut two pieces of vinyl-coated fabric, each 5-3/4" x 8-3/4".

4 Using the inside pages as a guide, punch three holes along one edge of both covers.

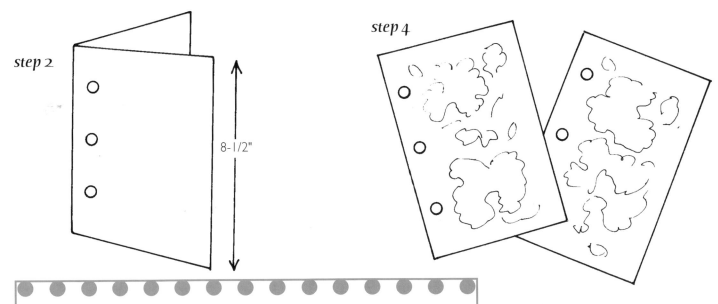

step 2

8-1/2"

step 4

TIP

If your barrettes or clips are too large to fit through one punched hole, punch two holes next to each other to allow enough space.

5 Open a barrette. Slip the back through the front cover, the inside pages, and the back cover. Snap shut. ❑

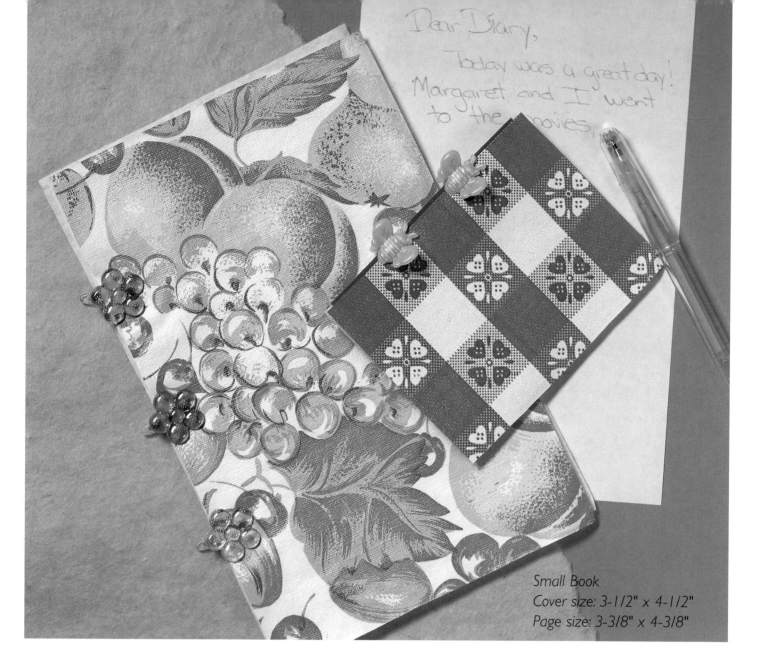

Small Book
Cover size: 3-1/2" x 4-1/2"
Page size: 3-3/8" x 4-3/8"

Smaller Book

SUPPLIES

• Vinyl fabric

• 2 sheets lightweight card-stock, 8-1/2" x 11"

• Small barrettes or clips

• 1/4" round hole punch

• Scissors, Ruler, Pencil

1 Measure and cut the paper to make 8 pages, each 3-3/8" x 4-3/8".

2 Punch two holes along the edge of one page about 1/4" from the edge. Using this page as your guide, punch two holes in the rest of the sheets.

3 Measure and cut two pieces of vinyl-coated fabric, each 3-1/2" x 4-1/2".

4 Using the inside pages as a guide, punch two holes along one edge of both covers.

5 Open a barrette or clip. Slip through the front cover, the inside pages, and the back cover. Snap shut. ❑

Tin Box Treasure Books

Oblong Tin Box

Box size: 3-3/4" x 2-1/2"

Book size: 3-1/8" x 1-7/8"

Round Tin Box

Box size: 2-1/2"

Book size: 2-1/4"

SUPPLIES

- Empty candy tins
- Craft foam pieces in assorted colors
- Glitter (fine is better)
- Double-sided tape
- Looseleaf fasteners (2 for each book)
- Hole punch
- Paper
- Shoe box lid
- Scissors, Ruler, Pencil

Decorate a candy tin with a craft-foam-and-glitter mosaic, then make a tiny treasure book to put inside. A mosaic is a surface decoration made by inlaying small pieces of various materials to a design. Traditional mosaics are made of glass or tile, but craft foam makes an easy, lightweight substitute. Be sure the tins are clean and dry before you start.

step 2

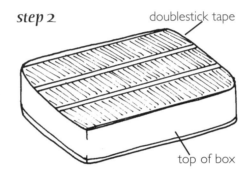

doublestick tape

top of box

step 3

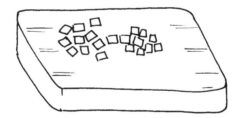

step 4

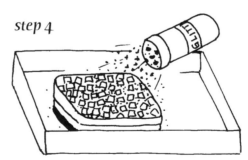

step 5

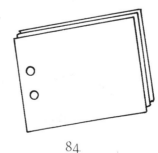

1 Cut tiny pieces of craft foam to create the design.

2 Create a sticky surface for the mosaic on the lid. Cover the top of the lid with double-sided tape, overlapping the strips, and trim around the edges.

3 Place the pieces of craft foam on the lid to form your design. Press them in place to make sure they're stuck.

4 Place the lid of the tin in a shoe box lid. Carefully sprinkle the tin lid with glitter, so the glitter fills the spaces between the foam pieces and covers the glue or tape. Tap off the extra glitter and return it to the glitter container.

5 Cut pages for a small book to fit inside the tin. Punch with a hole punch and bind with looseleaf fasteners. ❏

Bookmarks

A handmade bookmark makes a wonderful, thoughtful addition to a purchased book. Here are some ideas for special ones. Use scraps of paper, posterboard, ribbons, and trims to make your bookmarks.

Pom-pom Bookmark

1. Cut cardboard or cardstock 6" x 1-1/2" and round the corners.
2. Punch a hole on each end with a decorative punch.
3. Decorate with a punched paper shape.
4. Loop a piece of cord (8") through one hole.
5. Glue a pom-pom to each end of the cord. ❏

Daisy Bookmark

1. Cut a piece of ribbon 10" long.
2. Glue two daisy appliques back to back, sandwiching the end of the ribbon between them.
3. Thread some beads on the other end of the ribbon. Knot the ribbon to keep the beads in place. ❏

Garden Bookmark

1. Remove some silk flower leaves from their stems and backings. (Ask permission first!)
2. Glue them end to end, overlapping them slightly, in a row.
3. Glue a flower at the top.
4. Glue a gem in the center of the flower. ❏

Tag Bookmark

1. Cut strips of colored paper with a straight or decorative scissors. From the same paper, punch five hearts.
2. Glue them to a paper tag.
3. Loop a piece of twine (10") through the hole in the tag.
4. Glue two paper shapes back-to-back on each end of the twine, sandwiching the twine between the shapes.
5. Glue the remaining punched shape to the tag.
6. Label with a marker. ❏

Button Bookmark

1. Cut a 9" piece of striped grosgrain ribbon.
2. Choose four buttons of different sizes to match the ribbon.
3. Glue the largest one to one side of the ribbon.
4. Glue the remaining buttons in a stack on the other side of the ribbon. Let the glue dry completely. ❏

Magic Wand Bookmark

1. Twist 5 chenille stems together, leaving 2" on one end untwisted.
2. Add beads to the untwisted ends.
3. Bend the ends to secure the beads. ❏

Hair Dangles Bookmark

Loop a beaded hair elastic at the end of a large paperclip. ❏

Snap Together Books

Here's another way to bind pages together – snaps! They're a fun way to hold together an album for school photos or a secret story book. When you bind the pages together with snaps, they swing out in a chain that can be hung on a wall or stacked and tied for safekeeping.

Snap-Together Storybook

Size: 2-3/4" x 2-7/8"

1 Cut cardstock 5-1/2" x 2-7/8" for the pages. Fold each in half to make a page 2-3/4" x 2-7/8".

2 Punch a hole in each folded page on opposite corners.

3 Snap the snaps through the holes, lining up two pages at a time. You can make the chain as long as you like.

4 Cut a 2-1/4" square of printed paper using decorative-edge scissors. Glue or tape it to the front of the book.

5 Cut a 1-3/4" square of plain paper using decorative edge scissors. Glue or tape on top of the printed paper.

6 On the plain paper square, make a title for the book with stick-on letters. ❑

step 1

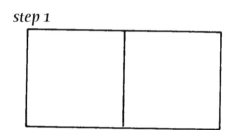

step 2

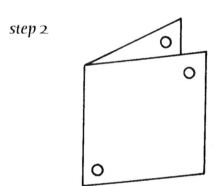

step 3

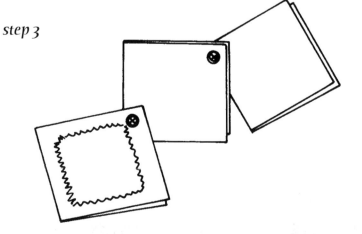

SUPPLIES

- Cardstock
- Hole punch
- Snaps (size no. 1 or larger) found in sewing stores
- Scraps of plain and decorative paper (to decorate the cover)
- Decorative-edge scissors
- Glue stick
- Stick-on letters
- Scissors, Pencil, Ruler

See page 90 for "Flower Petal Snap Together Book" instructions.

Flower Petal Snap Together Photo Album

Pictured on page 89   *Size: 4" diameter*

SUPPLIES

- Cardstock in three colors
- Snaps (size no. 1 or larger)
- Photos or color photocopies of photos
- Scraps of colored or patterned decorative paper
- 3/4 yd. thin cord
- Hole punch
- Glue stick or double stick tape
- Waterproof ink pen
- Scissors, Pencil, Ruler

1 Use the pattern provided to cut flower-shaped pages from cardstock.

2 Punch holes as shown on the pattern for the snaps.

3 Line up the holes in two pages and snap the snaps through the holes. Continue until you've attached all the pages with snaps.

4 Cut the photos in circles. Glue one photo at the center of each flower.

5 Decorate the cover with circles cut from decorative paper.

6 Using the pen, write your friends' names below their photos and write a title on the front of your book.

7 Arrange the pages so the petals stack up. Tie with a thin cord. ❑

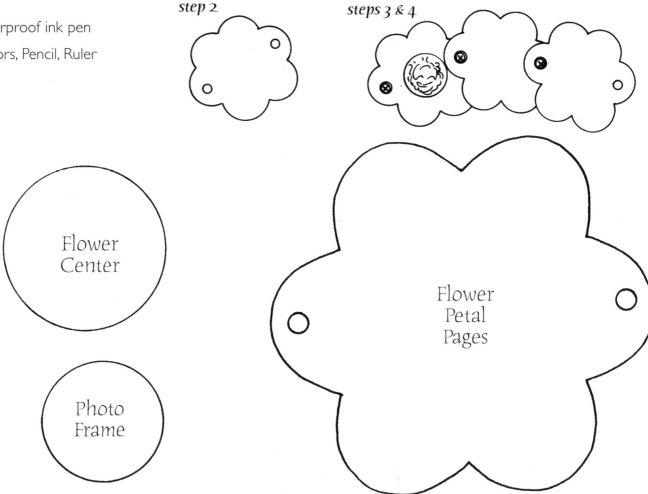

step 2

steps 3 & 4

Flower Center

Photo Frame

Flower Petal Pages

Secret Message Paper Chain Books

Write your secrets on strips of paper, then fold the strips and loop them together. The secrets are safely hidden and only you know what they are. You could even make a chain of "good works" coupons for your mom. She'll be surprised every time she removes a link from her chain and reads your secret surprise!

SUPPLIES

- Paper for chain links, thin paper works best
- Ball key chain and clip (optional)
- Ribbon (optional)
- Scissors, ruler, pencil

1 Cut paper strips in any of the sizes listed below. The bigger the pieces of paper, the bigger the chain. Cut as many pieces of paper you like to make the length of your chain – but they all have to be the same size.

1-1/2" × 3-1/2"	1-3/4 × 4"
2" × 4-3/4"	3" × 7"
3-3/4" × 8-1/2"	

2 Fold each strip in half the lengthwise, crease it, then unfold it.

3 Fold the two long sides in toward the center crease.

4 Fold along the center crease again. You now have a long thin piece of paper.

5 Fold the long piece in half and crease. Unfold.

6 Fold the two short ends to the center.

7 Fold again at center crease.

8 Make as many links as you want.

9 To link the pieces together, push the arms of one link in between the folds of another link. ❏

step 2

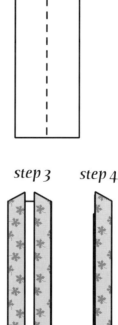

step 3 *step 4*

step 5 *step 6*

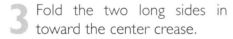

step 7 *step 9*

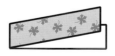

File Card Address Books

File cards – sold in office supply stores, stationery stores, and even drugstores – can be used to create a colorful address book. (If you combine different colors, your book will have a rainbow effect.)

Decorate the front with a few stickers and you've got a fun, inexpensive place to record information about the stars in your life.

Alphabet Indexed Address Book

Size: 6" x 4"

SUPPLIES

- Pink and lavender lined 4x6 index cards, 27 in all

- Alphabet tabbed cards, the size that goes with 4x6 cards

- Double-stick tape, 1/2" wide

- Stickers - Stars, hearts

- Permanent fine tip marker and white paper

- Scissors, Pencil, Ruler

1 Set aside one lavender card and two pink cards. Place remaining colored file cards between the alphabet tabbed cards, with the lined sides up.

2 Tape the stack together with double-stick tape, lining up the tape along the left side of the cards.

step 2

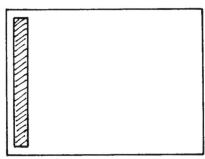

step 4

3 Tape the lavender card to the front of the "A" alphabet card. This is the front cover.

4 Wrap one of the pink cards around the left edge of the book and secure with double-stick tape.

5 Tape a pink card to the last card. This is the back cover.

6 Handwrite "Addresses & Phone numbers" on white paper or print out using your computer and printer.

7 Cut out the words. Glue on the cover.

8 Decorate the cover with stickers. ❑

See page 94 for "Binder Clip and Binder Ring Address Book" instructions.

Binder Clip Address Book

1 Trim the 10 green 4x6 cards so they are 3" x 6". These are the alphabet dividers.

2 Put two silver stars on the first green card. It is also the front cover). Use the ABC stickers to mark the green divider cards. Use three letters on all the cards except the last one

3 Stack the cards, starting with a green card, then three 3x5 cards, then another green card, then three 3x5 cards, and so on, putting a blank green card at the end until you've used all the cards.

4 Tape the cards together along the left hand edge of the stack with double-stick tape.

5 Place the binder clip on the left edge. ❑

step 1

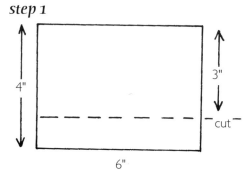

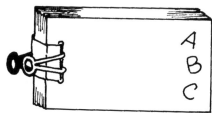

SUPPLIES

- 10 green 4x6 index cards
- 26 white 3x5 index cards
- Double-stick tape
- Stickers - White 3/4" ABCs, 1-1/2" silver stars
- White binder clip
- Scissors, Pencil, Ruler

Binder Ring Address Book

Size: 2" x 4"

1 Cut the 4x6 cards in thirds, so they are 2" x 4".

2 Punch a hole in the corner of each.

3 Make a stack of 28 cards.

4 Tape or glue the cards along the top. Avoid the holes.

5 Add a letter to each page, skipping the top card.

6 Trim off the bottom of the front card with pinking scissors so the letter "A" is visible.

step 1

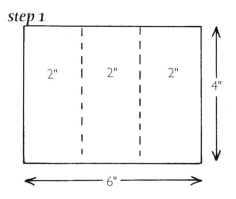

step 2

7 Decorate the front with a silver star sticker.

8 Put the binder ring through the holes.

9 Add the ball chain to the binder ring. ❑

SUPPLIES

- 10 colored 4x6 index cards
- Double-stick tape *or* glue stick
- Stickers - 1/2" black ABCs, 1-1/2" silver star
- Binder ring, 1-1/4"
- Pinking scissors
- Hole punch
- Silver ball keychain
- Scissors, Pencil, Ruler

About the Author

Janet Pensiero

Janet Pensiero began her career in Art at an early age when she taught herself to draw by tracing comics from the newspaper. Luckily, her parents recognized her unusual talents, and gave her art lessons, and lots of crayons and paper. After a childhood filled with arts and crafts of all kinds, she went to Moore College of Art in Philadelphia, got a degree and launched into the world of Design. Since then she's designed all kinds of things—from signs and Zoo exhibits to Toys and Christmas ornaments. For a while she even worked at a web site designing craft projects. These days she works for several different companies doing product development and design, and contributes to books and magazines on a regular basis. She even co-authored a book about memory crafts.

Using all the experiences she's had in the world of Art and Design, she's always in her studio in Philadelphia making something new. In fact, she came up with too many projects to fit in this book!

Metric Conversion Chart

Inches to Millimeters and Centimeters

Inches	MM	CM	Inches	MM	CM
1/8	3	.3	2	51	5.1
1/4	6	.6	3	76	7.6
3/8	10	1.0	4	102	10.2
1/2	13	1.3	5	127	12.7
5/8	16	1.6	6	152	15.2
3/4	19	1.9	7	178	17.8
7/8	22	2.2	8	203	20.3
1	25	2.5	9	229	22.9
1-1/4	32	3.2	10	254	25.4
1-1/2	38	3.8	11	279	27.9
1-3/4	44	4.4	12	305	30.5

Yards to Meters

Yards	Meters	Yards	Meters
1/8	.11	3	2.74
1/4	.23	4	3.66
3/8	.34	5	4.57
1/2	.46	6	5.49
5/8	.57	7	6.40
3/4	.69	8	7.32
7/8	.80	9	8.23
1	.91	10	9.14
2	1.83		

Index